The Politics of Immigration

The Politics of Immigration
Questions and Answers

Jane Guskin and David L. Wilson

Monthly Review Press
New York

Library of Congress Cataloging-in-Publication Data

Guskin, Jane.
   The politics of immigration : questions and answers / Jane Guskin and David L.
Wilson.
      p. cm.
   Includes bibliographical references and index.
   ISBN-13: 978-1-58367-155-9
   ISBN-13: 978-1-58367-156-6
   1. United States--Emigration and immigration. 2. United States--Emigration and immi-
gration--Government policy. 3. Immigrants--United States. 4. Immigrants--Government
policy--United States. I. Wilson, David L. (David Leigh), 1946- II. Title.
   JV6465.G87 2007
   325.73--dc22
                                      2007017332
   Design: Terry J. Allen

MONTHLY REVIEW FOUNDATION
146 West 29ᵗʰ Street – Suite 6W
New York, NY 10001

http://www.monthlyreview.org

Table of Contents

1195

122950

Dedication

This book is dedicated with respect and admiration to all immigrants and their families who are resisting deportation, discrimination, exploitation, and oppression.

Acknowledgments

We thank John Mage and Carol Skelskey at Monthly Review Press for suggesting the idea for this book and trusting us to write it, and the whole team at Monthly Review for their support and patience. Jane gives special thanks to her parents, Sam and Phyllis Guskin, for their encouragement, support and feedback, and to her husband, Esneider Arevalo, for his inspiration and understanding. Our sincere appreciation goes to all the people who took the time to review the manuscript and share their thoughts and suggestions: Amy Gottlieb (of the American Friends Service Committee), Amy Sugimori (of the National Employment Law Project, now at La Fuente, a Tri-State Worker & Community Fund), Carter Wilson, David B. Wilson, Aarti Shahani (of Families for Freedom), Ken Estey, Arnoldo Garcia (of National Network of Immigrant and Refugee Rights), David Bacon, Mark Dow, Anthony Arnove, and Will Coley. While their feedback helped us shape the text, they are not to blame for any errors or shortcomings.

Preface:

Is the United States a Nation of Immigrants?

It's often said that the United States is a country built by immigrants. It's true that the nation was founded by recent arrivals to this land—at the expense of the original inhabitants (Native Americans), and with the slave labor of people brought here by force from Africa. It's also true that a majority of the country's current population are descendants of immigrants.

Certainly, immigration is not new to this country. Why, then, does each successive wave of newcomers spark so much controversy?

As this book goes to press, immigration is again a major political issue. Raids and detention are on the rise, tearing apart families and communities. Congress is promising tougher enforcement, and maybe a "guest worker" program, to keep immigrants in their place.

Resistance is also swelling, and taking new forms. In the spring of 2006, immigrants and their supporters hit the streets with massive demonstrations. Hundreds of thousands of people, of all ages and colors, marched with U.S. flags and signs reading "We Are America."

A year later, churches are banding together to forge a new "sanctuary" movement, framing it as an explicitly political act in support of immigrants and their families. Communities respond to raids with outrage, and public expressions of solidarity. Organizations across the country sponsor a "night of 1,000 conversations" to discuss immigration.

Every day, more people are realizing that immigrants are here to stay. They are our friends, our parents, our partners, our neighbors, ourselves. Either we condemn them to live as a permanent underclass, or we look for ways to integrate them into a more just and inclusive society.

As the Los Angeles–based rapper Jae-P puts it in his song "Vecino" (Neighbor):

I don't come to beg, or for you to give me anything
I come for the dollar, and to provide for my family
Your country is big and needs me
If there wasn't work, we wouldn't be here
Remember, your grandparents did my job
They came as immigrants searching for the same thing
Study the history of this country
You'll see that everyone came to build

I know you like me, you eat my food
I know you like me, you ask me for help
Don't be afraid of me if I don't look like you
If I take off my skin, I'm exactly like you
I'm your neighbor and will always be
Learn Spanish and I'll learn English
So we can understand each other much better
Together we can pull this great nation forward
                        —Jae-P, "Vecino" (Excerpts translated
                        into English by Jane Guskin)

Authors' Notes

Where did these questions come from?

People who are uncomfortable with immigration, or with certain kinds of immigrants, often raise specific objections to make their case. Even though these arguments are largely based on myths, they can spread seeds of doubt in the minds of many people who are unsure about immigration, because they tap into real fears about jobs, wages, and changing communities. Well-funded anti-immigrant organizations and politicians try to exploit these fears to gain political advantage.

Advocates of immigrant rights often hesitate to directly address negative rhetoric, preferring to take a positive approach. And those of us with strong pro-immigrant opinions sometimes lack the tools we need to effectively counter anti-immigrant myths when they emerge from the mouths of co-workers, family members, neighbors, or friends.

The idea of this book is to address people's real fears with facts and honest arguments, to encourage everyone to take a deeper and broader look at immigration and its root causes, and to suggest some possible courses of action. We hope this book will reach the doubters—those people with genuine concerns about immigration—and be a useful source for immigrants and their supporters seeking to foster public dialogue around the issue.

Who are we talking to?

We hope this book is read by all kinds of people: immigrants and U.S.-born citizens, people with and without legal immigration status. We have alternated between referring to these different groups of readers as "you," "we," or "they" at various times over the course of the book. This is not meant to offend or exclude anyone, or to distance ourselves from anyone, but rather to acknowledge the diversity of our readers and encourage them to occasionally step into someone else's shoes, and see things from a different perspective.

Caveat

This book is *not* designed to explain to immigrants how they can legalize their status in the United States. That would require a whole book about immigration law, and it would undoubtedly be out of date before it even got to the publisher. As readers will likely notice, at the date of publication there are very few avenues open to people trying to legalize their status. Anyone who wants to know if they qualify should consult a reliable lawyer or legal service agency for advice. Try to get referrals from trusted friends or community-based organizations—there are unfortunately a lot of people out there who will be happy to charge a fee and promise to get you legal documents. If you're not careful, you may lose your money and end up in deportation proceedings.

Terminology

We use several terms in this book to describe people who are living in the United States without permission from the federal government. "Out of status" is the most accurate term, and reflects the transitory nature of immigration status—but it is sometimes awkward, especially when used repeatedly. "Undocumented" is more popularly used in the United States, and is relatively neutral. In Europe, the term "without papers" is common. (Occasionally we use "illegal," in quotes, just to make sure everyone understands that what so many people call "illegal" is what we are referring to as out of status or undocumented.)

As of April 1, 1997, to conform with laws passed in 1996, the immigration agency began using the term "removal" instead of "deportation" to describe the process of sending immigrants back to their home countries. Removal is a more legally precise term, but deportation is more widely recognized and understood. In this book we use the terms interchangeably.

1

Who Are the Immigrants?

How do we define immigrants?

Immigrants are people who move from one country to another in order to settle there. U.S. government agencies distinguish between immigrants, visitors, and "non-immigrants," including temporary workers and foreign students. But in reality, some "non-immigrants" come planning to settle down, while others plan to leave but end up staying.

The government and many journalists use the term "alien" to cover all the different types of people who come here. Demographers—people who study populations and how they change—prefer to call them "foreign born," because "alien" also means strange and different.

Demographers use the term "authorized migrants" or "authorized immigrants" to refer to foreign-born people living in the United States with a legal status recognized by the federal government. People living here without permission from the federal government are "out-of-status immigrants" or "undocumented immigrants." The government and the media usually prefer to call them "unauthorized aliens," "illegal aliens," "illegal immigrants," or just "illegals"—perhaps because terms like these make it easier to dehumanize people and to justify denying their human rights. At a meeting with immigration officers after the arrests of immigrant workers at a factory in Wisconsin in the summer of 2006, Sandra Jiménez, an authorized migrant from Mexico, asked an immigration officer to stop calling the detainees "illegal aliens." "The word makes me think of strange little creatures," Jiménez said. "I am not a Martian."[1]

The word "migrants" can also refer to people who move from one area to another within their own country. Over the decades following the Civil War, millions of African Americans fled oppressive conditions in the rural South to seek a better life in northern cities, or in the West.[2] Because the United States had been reunited, these migrants didn't have to cross a national border, so they weren't immigrants. If the war had ended differently, African Americans might have had to cross into another country in order to escape— just as some 20,000 to 30,000 of them did between 1820 and 1860, fleeing slavery in the South and dodging bounty hunters in the northern states to reach freedom in Canada through the "underground railroad."[3]

How many immigrants are here?

As of 2004, there were about 25.4 million "authorized migrants" living in the United States. About two-fifths of them—11.4 million—had become naturalized citizens. About 10.4 million had lawful permanent resident status (commonly known as "having a green card" because the ID card used to be green). About 2.5 million migrants had refugee or asylum status—they fled their home countries because of persecution and had not yet become permanent residents. About 1.1 million people were "temporary legal residents," people living in the United States as temporary workers, students, or diplomats.[4]

It's harder to figure out how many people are living here out of status. Most estimates now are based on a "residual method," where we take the number of foreign-born people counted in the surveys or by the U.S. Census Bureau, and then subtract the number of authorized migrants reported by immigration authorities. Demographers know that some out-of-status immigrants avoid census takers, so they add a certain percentage back in to compensate for the undercount.

In 2005, a careful study published by the Migration Policy Institute (MPI), a nonprofit research group in Washington, D.C., estimated there were 10.3 million immigrants living in the United States without papers in 2004.[5] In

2006, Jeffrey Passel, a researcher for the Pew Hispanic Center, another Washington nonprofit, estimated that the out-of-status population had grown to 11.1 million in 2005 and was between 11.5 million and 12 million in 2006.[6]

Are immigrants different from other people?

Compared to the general population, a larger proportion of immigrants are young adults, since immigrants tend to come here when they are at prime working age—that is, between twenty and fifty-four years old.[7]

In terms of family income, there's not much difference between authorized migrants and U.S.-born citizens. In 2003, the average annual income for a household headed by an authorized migrant was $47,800 a year, while the average income for families headed by someone born here was $47,700. Average income was far lower for households headed by out-of-status immigrants: $27,400.[8]

Compared to the general U.S. population, a larger proportion of immigrants trace their roots to Latin America or Asia. The top ten countries of origin for the 1,122,373 people who became legal permanent residents in 2005 were Mexico, India, China, the Philippines, Cuba, Vietnam, the Dominican Republic, Korea, Colombia, and Ukraine.[9] The result has been a demographic shift over the past forty years; data compiled by the *New York Times* from the Census Bureau and other sources showed that 56.6 percent of the U.S. population in 2006 was "non-Hispanic" white, down from 76.6 percent in 1967.[10]

Who are the undocumented immigrants?

Many people assume all out-of-status immigrants are Mexican, or at least "Latino" or "Hispanic." In fact, Mexicans *are* a majority: in 2004, nearly 57 percent of the 10.3 million out-of-status immigrants had come from Mexico—nearly six million people. Some 24 percent, about 2.5 million people, were from Central and South America and the Caribbean. Asia accounted for an estimated one million people (9 percent), Europe for 600,000 (nearly 6 percent), and Africa for 400,000 (nearly 4 percent).[11]

People sometimes assume all out-of-status immigrants "jumped the border." According to U.S. government estimates, about 60 percent come here without permission ("enter without inspection," in immigration jargon): they slip across the Mexican or Canadian border in secret, take a boat from a Caribbean island, or enter via other means with false papers. But 40 percent, or two out of five, enter with permission and then fail to leave when their visas expire—they become "overstays."[12]

About 75 percent of undocumented workers are employed in the formal economy; the rest work "off the books." Contrary to the stereotypes, relatively few of the undocumented do farm work—about 4.2 percent, as of 2000— although many did in the past, and undocumented workers still made up about 24 percent of the fewer than one million agricultural workers in the United States in 2000. About 20 percent of out-of-status workers were in manufacturing in 2000, 16 percent in leisure or hospitality, and 13 percent in construction. Not all were in low-level jobs—11.5 percent worked as managers or professionals.[13]

Is there a "new wave" of immigration?

In 2004, the U.S. population was about 293 million, according to the U.S. Census Bureau. By the Migration Policy Institute's estimate, a total of 35.7 million foreign-born people were living here that year, including some 11.4 million naturalized citizens. That means about one in eight people—about 12.8 percent of the total population—was from somewhere else. The undocumented were 29 percent of the immigrant population, or 3.5 percent of the entire U.S. population.

In 1965, 4.4 percent of the total population in the United States was foreign born. The proportion of immigrants rose gradually to 6.2 percent in 1980, then more rapidly to 7.9 percent in 1990 and to 11.1 percent in 2000.[14] The foreign-born population was 19.8 million in 1990; it jumped to 31.1 million by 2000, a 57 percent increase.[15] (Other studies put the increase somewhat lower—a jump of 9.1 million, or 46 percent.)[16]

The 1990–2000 growth rate was even faster for out-of-status immigrants. Their number rose at an annual rate of 500,000 a year, more than doubling from 3.5 million in 1990 to 8.5 million in 2000.[17]

Is the new wave really new?

At 12.8 percent, the proportion of immigrants in the population as of 2004 was about the same as it's been for most of U.S. history. Foreign-born people made up 9.7 percent of the population in 1850 and rose to 14.7 percent in 1910.[18] The rise in the immigrant population from 1990 to 2000 was much less dramatic than the one from 1901 to 1910, when the population was just ninety-two million and the number of immigrants had jumped by 8.8 million.[19]

Anti-immigrant sentiment swelled in the early 1900s as many native-born citizens began to fear they'd be overwhelmed by the flow of "darker" Europeans—Italians, Greeks, Poles, and Russian Jews. But the First World War cut down the influx from Europe, and in 1924 anti-immigrant forces succeeded in getting Congress to pass the National Origins Act, which severely restricted immigration from Southern and Eastern Europe, while continuing the exclusion of Asians. This is why the proportion of the foreign born was unusually low in 1960.[20]

The new wave may seem larger to many people now because immigrants are increasingly moving to small towns and suburbs, particularly in southeastern and midwestern states. Most immigrants still settle in California, New York, Texas, Florida, New Jersey, and Illinois, mainly in urban areas where they tend to blend in with the general population. But the numbers going to other states increased dramatically from 2000 to 2005—by 34 percent in Indiana, 44 percent in South Dakota, 32 percent in Delaware, and 31 percent in Missouri.[21]

Are politicians stirring up a panic about immigration?

In November 1973, under President Richard Nixon, former marine officer Leonard F. Chapman took office as commissioner of the Immigration and Naturalization Service (INS). Chapman told congressional committees in 1976 that there were at least six to seven million out-of-status immigrants in the United States at that time, and maybe as many as ten to twelve million. On January 17, 1972, the weekly *US News & World Report* warned its readers: "Never have so many aliens swarmed illegally into United States—millions, moving across the nation. For government, they are becoming a costly headache." According to a December 29, 1974, *New York Times* article on the "silent invasion," one million immigrants lived in the New York metropolitan area alone at that time. On June 23, 1976, a *New Orleans Times-Picayune* headline announced "Illegal Aliens: They Invade U.S. 8.2 Million Strong," On August 26, 1982, the *Saginaw News* in Michigan reported: "As many as 15 million are already here."

In fact, a study by Census Bureau demographers concluded in 1980 that the number that year was "almost certainly below 6 million, and may be substantially less, possibly only 3.5 to 5 million."[22]

Some people get alarmed when they see newcomers in their communities. Xenophobia, or "fear of foreigners," may be a common response, but it has a negative impact—creating rifts between communities and slowing the pace of social integration. The alternative is to seek out options that will help us adapt to changing demographics and allow us to forge a more inclusive identity.

2

Why Do People Immigrate?

What are the "root causes" of migration?

Some people are nomadic and don't settle down in one place for any length of time. But most people prefer to remain in one area and build a stable community there. Sometimes people are uprooted from their homes by violence, or by economic, social, or political pressures. This "forced displacement" can push people from rural areas into cities or refugee camps, from one region to another, or across borders into other countries.

The Irish potato famine of the mid-1800s led about one million Irish people to seek survival elsewhere; hundreds of thousands came to the United States. The first wave of Asian immigration to the United States was largely people fleeing China to escape the violence that accompanied the Taiping Rebellion (1850–1864).[1] Many Jews came here to escape the anti-Semitic pogroms of Tsarist Russia in the late nineteenth and early twentieth centuries.

Millions of people continue to migrate because their communities are devastated by poverty and violence. For others, it may be possible to survive in their communities, but by migrating they can get jobs that pay more, allowing them to seek a better future for their families. Many migrants hope to return home as soon as economic and political conditions in their homeland improve. Often these hopes are dashed, as conditions only worsen, and family members left behind increasingly depend on their support for basic needs.

Any of us might make the decision to migrate if we faced similar conditions. "I'm a retired cop," said a Long Island man during a public meeting shown in the 2003 award-winning documentary *Farmingville*. "I was in the Marine Corps. I have a lot of respect for the laws of the United States. If I lived in Mexico and I knew I had some advantage here to help my family back in Mexico, I'd be wading across the Rio Grande myself. I'd be on a raft floating from Haiti, I'd be crossing the border from Yugoslavia into Germany. I'd be going into England. I'd do anything I can to help my family."[2]

Why do people come to the United States?

Many people consider the United States to be a land of freedom and opportunity, and believe that people from around the world are eager to come here. But for most people who are driven to migrate, a combination of three main factors influences where they choose to go: economic opportunities in the destination country; the presence of family or friends there who can help them get a job and a place to live; and the distance, difficulty, and expense of the trip.

The United States has a large economy with a range of job opportunities, and many material goods are cheaper here, relative to income levels, than in other countries. Our history as an immigrant nation means many foreign citizens have family or friends—or even entire communities from their homeland—already living here, to help the newcomers adjust. And compared to Western Europe, the United States is easier to reach for most migrants from Mexico, Central and South America, the Caribbean, and eastern Asia. (Immigrants from Africa and western Asia often prefer to go to Europe.)

Some immigrants are drawn to the United States because it promises certain freedoms, like freedom of speech and of religion. And despite continuing economic and social inequalities in the United States, and racial discrimination, immigrants sometimes feel they can leave behind the class and caste prejudices of their home countries and make a fresh start here.

Is it our fault other countries have so many problems?

In recent decades, immigrants to the United States have come largely from places where the U.S. government has carried out major military, political, or economic interventions, such as Mexico, the Philippines, Cuba, Vietnam, the Dominican Republic, Korea, Central America, and Haiti. We share the blame for our government's foreign policies if we do nothing to oppose them.

In the 1980s, U.S.-backed wars against leftist revolutionary movements in Central America left some 300,000 people dead—about one out of every hundred inhabitants. The United States continues to spend billions of dollars on a similar armed strategy in Colombia, where government forces are trying to crush a more than forty-year-old insurgency. The U.S. government also trains Latin American military officers who have been accused of abducting, torturing, and murdering civilians throughout the hemisphere.

The United States likewise bears a large share of responsibility for most of the economic crises that have sparked mass migration since the 1980s. These crises have their roots in economic policies which are dictated either directly by the U.S. government through its regional "free trade" agreements, or indirectly through U.S.-dominated international lending institutions like the World Bank, the International Monetary Fund (IMF), and the World Trade Organization (WTO).

The IMF and the World Bank function by making loans to already heavily indebted countries, on the condition that their governments follow an economic model promoted by U.S. economists and the media as "open markets," "free trade," and "globalization." Analysts in Latin America and much of the rest of the world call this model "neoliberalism." (This comes from the old sense of "liberalism," which referred to the free trade policies of classical economists like Adam Smith and David Ricardo.)

The neoliberal model and its "structural adjustment" plans involve sharply reducing the supply of currency; selling off state-owned industries and services to private companies; scaling back and privatizing healthcare, education, and other social programs; and eliminating or sharply reducing tariffs that protect domestic industries and agriculture. Such measures generally reduce inflation and stabilize currency exchange rates, but at the cost of shrinking real wages, high unemployment rates, an expansion of poverty, and the wholesale destruction of small-scale agriculture—which causes precisely the kind of economic devastation that leads so many people to migrate.

Why do so many Mexicans come here?

After its 1910 revolution, Mexico grew from a primarily agricultural country to what in 2005 was the thirteenth largest economy in the world, right behind India and ahead of Russia. Its economic growth rate was as high as 6 percent a year. Poorer Mexicans were often excluded from the benefits of this growth, but life did improve for many people; the illiteracy rate was cut in half and mortality rates fell dramatically.[3]

In the early 1980s, Mexico suffered a financial crisis brought on by a worldwide recession and the government's over-borrowing during the 1970s oil boom. To get out of the crisis, the government started implementing a neoliberal economic model. Proponents of the change claimed that unemployment and other dislocations caused by these policies would be more than made up for by foreign investment, expanded trade, and a rapid expansion of industrial jobs in the *maquiladoras*—the largely tax-exempt assembly plants producing goods for export, including the factories that line Mexico's border with the United States.

Mexico forged ahead with the plan, signing a letter of intent to sell off 1,200 state-owned companies in 1984, and then amending the Mexican constitution in 1992 to allow the privatization of many *ejidos*, the *campesino*-controlled cooperative farms that were the heart of Mexico's agrarian reform in the 1930s.[4]

In the early 1990s, the government of Carlos Salinas de Gortari negotiated a model neoliberal trade accord with the United States and Canada—the North American Free Trade Agreement, better known as NAFTA.

Mexico's economy had shown no sign of recovery by the time NAFTA went into effect on January 1, 1994, but the United States promoted the Mexican experience as an example for the rest of Latin America. In December 1994, U.S. president Bill Clinton hosted a "Summit of the Americas" in Miami, with thirty-four heads of state meeting to ratify a plan for a Free Trade Area of the Americas, which was supposed to extend NAFTA to the whole hemisphere by

2005. Two weeks later, the Mexican peso collapsed. On January 31, 1995, fearing a total collapse of the Mexican economy that would affect a large number of U.S. investors, Clinton put together a $49 billion bailout package for Mexico.

Under NAFTA and WTO policies that forced the reduction or elimination of protective tariffs, more than 1.5 million Mexican farmers have lost their sources of income and have been forced to sell or abandon their farms. Consumer prices were supposed to decline under NAFTA—yet while the prices paid to farmers for their products have plummeted, consumer food prices have risen in all three NAFTA countries. As of 2005, Mexican farmers earned 70 percent less for their corn than they did before NAFTA, while Mexicans paid 50 percent more for tortillas. Without the protection of tariffs, Mexico became increasingly dependent on food imports: in 1995 the country's grain imports jumped from five to seven million tons a year to ten million tons. The dependence on imports means that when exchange rates fluctuate real food prices can double or triple.[5]

Far from producing the jobs and trade promised, the neoliberal model landed Mexico in an even bigger economic crisis, one that cost Mexican workers 751,041 jobs in the first eight months of 1995—more than the 648,000 maquiladora jobs Mexico had acquired by then.[6] Meanwhile, the real purchasing power of the Mexican minimum wage fell by more than two-thirds from 1980 to 1996.[7]

The biggest impact on immigration from Mexico has been from the rising gap between Mexican and U.S. wages. Up to the 1970s, Mexican workers were paid about one-fourth to one-third of what their U.S. counterparts got. (The cost of living is generally lower in Mexico, although some items cost as much as in the United States or even more.) Wages dropped drastically in the 1980s, and by the late 1990s workers in Mexico were making about one-eighth what they would be making for the same job in the United States; in some occupations the Mexican workers are now paid one-fifteenth what they would get north of the border.[8]

In 1981, a Mexican factory worker could have gotten three or four times as much money by crossing the border; not necessarily enough of a difference to make up for the risks and hardships of immigration. Just a few years later, the same factory worker's actual purchasing power had dropped to about one-third of its previous level—but now the worker could get paid eight to fifteen times as much by going to the U.S.

Why don't people stay home and fix their own countries?

In the 2001 documentary *Uprooted: Refugees of the Global Economy*, "Maricel," an immigrant from the Philippines, tells how she ended up going overseas as a domestic worker. Seeing ads everywhere encouraging people to work abroad, and facing a lack of opportunities at home, Maricel made a tough decision. "I realized that it's just a waste of time for me to go to college," she said, "because those people who went to college, they wasted four years studying hard, and then they have to go abroad to work as domestics. And I said that I just don't want to waste any more time...I'm just going to go abroad."

As of July 2006, the Philippines had a total foreign debt of more than $35 billion. "On top of that the economy is not doing well, and you have this loan that [has] to be paid off, and people are talking about even like ten generations will pass and we won't be able to survive," explains Maricel. "So, realistically speaking, when is it going to be better? Is there a possibility that the economy gets better? You're paying the debt, and on top of it you have this big, big interest. It's not very realistic that you will come out of it, like the Philippines will come out of it in one piece." With no opportunities in her home country, Maricel ended up in New York City, and eventually became an organizer helping other domestic workers fight exploitation.[9]

When people have no hope that things will get better, they are more likely to uproot themselves and go elsewhere to survive. If they believe they can improve the situation in their countries, they are less inclined to leave—and if things do get better, many will return home.

Starting in 1910, an estimated one to one and a half million Mexicans crossed the northern border to escape the violence of the Mexican revolution. Mexico's population was about fifteen million at the time, so this was a major migration—almost one out of every ten Mexicans.[10] But many returned to Mexico once the violence let up, and the revolution opened new opportunities back home, including social programs such as a sweeping agrarian reform, which handed out small farm plots to landless peasants.

What happens when people do try to fix their countries?

In the Central American nation of Nicaragua, an earthquake struck on December 23, 1972, killing as many as 10,000 people and destroying about 80 percent of the buildings in the capital city, Managua. The country's U.S.-backed dictator, Anastasio Somoza Debayle, funneled much of the international aid into his own family's pockets, leaving the population without help. Yet the disaster did not provoke a massive wave of migration. A movement to overthrow Somoza had been building for the past decade, and many Nicaraguans stayed home to push for change.

Washington continued to support Somoza, despite the earthquake aid debacle and a series of worsening human rights abuses, but in the end it could no longer prop him up against widespread opposition. On July 19, 1979, an insurrection led by the leftist Sandinista National Liberation Front (FSLN) toppled Somoza and began to transform Nicaragua from a dictator's feudal estate into a real country, with political pluralism and a "mixed economy"—based on the economic models of countries like France and Sweden, which combine public and private ownership of important economic sectors.

Nicaragua's real Gross Domestic Product (GDP) grew by a total of 7.67 percent per capita from 1979 to 1983, while the real GDP fell by 14.71 percent per capita for Central America as a whole.[11] But with fierce anti-communist Ronald Reagan as president, the U.S. government decided it couldn't live with the way Nicaraguans were fixing their country, and it started funneling money, weapons, training, and other "assistance" to recruit local fighters, known as the *contras,* for a proxy war that targeted civilian supporters of the Sandinista government. The war halted economic progress. Eleven years and some 30,000 deaths later, the United States won its war of attrition when Nicaraguans, tired of fighting, voted the FSLN out of office.

For all their struggles and sacrifice, Nicaraguans were cheated out of the chance to fix their country. The new U.S.-backed government quickly imposed

IMF-sponsored "structural adjustment" programs that brought a sharp rise in unemployment and triggered a recession, plunging the already impoverished population into desperate misery. Many Nicaraguans fled to neighboring Costa Rica. Costa Rica's 1984 census counted 45,918 Nicaraguans; by 2000 the country had 226,374 Nicaraguan residents, two-thirds of whom said they had arrived during the 1990s.[12]

In El Salvador and Guatemala, the U.S. government backed right-wing regimes as they tried to crush revolutionary leftist movements similar to Nicaragua's. These wars ended with peace accords—in 1992 in El Salvador and in 1996 in Guatemala—that allowed the leftist forces to regroup as political parties. But 70,000 Salvadorans and 200,000 Guatemalans had been killed, the vast majority of them by the U.S.-backed regimes, which remained in power and began imposing neoliberal economic programs. The wars left deep wounds in the countries' social and economic fabric. As of 2005, El Salvador's homicide rate of fifty-four murders per 100,000 people was by far the highest in Latin America;[13] nearly half the rural population lived below the poverty line, and 61 percent had no access to water piped into the home.[14]

During the worst of the fighting, in the 1980s, the number of Nicaraguans living in the United States, with or without permission, jumped from 44,166 to 168,659, according to the U.S. Census. The number of Salvadorans rose from 94,447 to 465,433; and Guatemalans went up from 63,073 to 225,739. The numbers rose almost as much during the 1990s, as neoliberal economic programs took effect in these countries: by 2000 there were 220,335 Nicaraguans, 817,336 Salvadorans, and 480,665 Guatemalans in the United States.[15]

Haitians suffered a similar fate. In December 1990, Haitians seized an opportunity for change, overwhelmingly electing popular priest Jean-Bertrand Aristide as president. Turnout was 80 percent of registered voters, with 67 percent voting for Aristide, compared to 13 percent for his closest competitor. Haitians hoped Aristide would carry out his promises to oppose IMF programs and raise the standard of living in the hemisphere's poorest country.

But less than a year later, in September 1991, Aristide was overthrown in a military coup. Army officers and right-wing paramilitaries linked to U.S. intelligence agencies unleashed massive repression against grassroots and leftist activists. Their hopes for change crushed, Haitians fled: U.S. Coast Guard data showed a notable drop of migrants fleeing Haiti by boat after the December 1990 elections, followed by a dramatic upturn after the 1991 coup.[16] According to the U.S. Census Bureau, 419,317 foreign-born Haitians were living in the United States in 2000, more than double the number living here a decade earlier.[17]

How can we address the root causes of immigration?

We can address the root causes of immigration and forced displacement by supporting people's efforts to build a better future in their own countries. We can oppose war, political violence and harmful economic policies, and take action in solidarity with workers throughout the world who are organizing to defend their rights.

During the 1980s, many thousands of people spoke out against U.S. intervention in Central America. Activists protested and lobbied Congress; many traveled to Central America to provide assistance and bring back information on conditions in the region, significantly undercutting the Reagan administration's efforts to depict Central American leftists as a threat to the United States. This activism had an impact on public opinion: by April 1986, a *New York Times*/CBS poll showed some 62 percent of U.S. respondents opposed financial aid to the *contras* in Nicaragua, while just 25 percent supported it.[18]

In the early 1990s, labor unions and activists led a campaign against NAFTA, and in 1999, giant protests erupted in Seattle against the WTO and its policies, sparking a new "anti-globalization" movement in the United States. These protests took their lead from workers in Latin America and elsewhere, who had long been out in the streets fighting the same policies. Mexicans organized innumerable marches, rallies, strikes, sit-ins, and occupations of government buildings; the Zapatistas, thousands of indigenous farmers who rose up in southern Mexico in 1994, started their rebellion on the day NAFTA went into effect, calling it a "death sentence" for indigenous people.

Over the past decade, campus and labor activists in the United States have built an anti-sweatshop movement which has made important gains in supporting successful local worker-organizing campaigns in Latin America and throughout the world. In 2001, for example, when workers were illegally fired for organizing at the KukDong factory in Atlixco de Puebla, Mexico—which produced goods for Nike and Reebok—a group called United Students Against Sweatshops (USAS) exerted enough pressure through its Sweat-Free Campus Campaign to force the companies to reinstate the fired workers. It was the first such reinstatement in over twenty years in Mexico, and marked a shift in power for independent organizing drives in the country's *maquiladoras*.[19]

In 2002 and 2003, USAS helped workers at the BJ&B factory in the town of Villa Altagracia, Dominican Republic, win the first union in a "Free Trade Zone" in the Caribbean in five years. "When workers first tried unionizing the BJ&B hat factory that is the town's biggest employer, the streets were abuzz with rumors that the factory would rather close down than negotiate," the *New York Times* reported. "Two years later, not only is the factory still around, but there also is a union, and it recently negotiated a labor contract that provides raises, scholarships, and other benefits that are unheard of among the country's 500 foreign-owned plants."[20] Such organizing victories give workers more control over their jobs and their lives, and ease the pressures that lead so many to migrate.

3

Does the United States Welcome Refugees?

What is a refugee?

Many people consider a refugee to be anyone who has fled his or her country to escape unbearable circumstances. Immigrants are sometimes described as "refugees of the global economy," to draw attention to the way economic conditions are displacing people from their homelands.

The 1951 United Nations Convention relating to the status of refugees describes a refugee in much narrower terms: someone who has left their country "owing to a well-founded fear of being persecuted for reasons of race, religion, nationality, membership of a particular social group, or political opinion," and whose government cannot or will not protect them. In 2005, the United Nations High Commissioner for Refugees (UNHCR) classified about 8.4 million of the world's 191 million migrants as refugees.

Refugee status is granted on a case-by-case basis to migrants who qualify. Sometimes, in the case of a mass exodus of civilians fleeing war or persecution—as with the Vietnamese "boat people"—the UNHCR declares "group" refugee status, in which all civilians in the group are considered refugees unless proven otherwise. Once granted status, refugees are often housed in crowded camps in neighboring nations under terrible conditions. After many years, some who have no hope of returning home are resettled permanently in another country. The United States is one of about eighteen nations that accepts and resettles refugees.

The Refugee Act of 1980 established two different categories: one for people who apply for refugee status from another country; and one for those who enter the United States and then apply for asylum. Like refugees, asylum seekers have the burden of proving "persecution or a well-founded fear of persecution on account of race, religion, nationality, membership in a particular social group, or political opinions" under a series of complex and strict rules. A year after entering the United States, refugees are expected to apply for permanent resident status; asylees may also seek permanent residency after a year.[1]

The Voyage of the *St. Louis*

Immigration from Europe dropped dramatically after Congress imposed new restrictions on European immigrants in 1924. But large numbers of Europeans tried to immigrate to the United States in the 1930s and 1940s despite the restrictions, mainly Jews and others fleeing the Nazi regime.

The United States admitted about 250,000 of these refugees from 1933 to 1941, including a large number of academics and professionals.[2] Many others were rejected. Some of these refugees were accepted by Mexico or Canada; many of them later crossed the border into the United States to join friends and relatives already living here.

Others weren't as fortunate. In May 1939, the German ocean liner *St. Louis* sailed from Hamburg to Havana with 937 passengers, most of them Jews seeking asylum from the Nazis. The majority planned to wait in Cuba while the U.S. government processed their applications for visas. But the Cuban government allowed only 28 passengers to land. The ship left Havana and sailed for Miami as the passengers cabled U.S. president Franklin Roosevelt asking to be accepted as refugees. The U.S. State Department answered that they had to "await their turns on the waiting list and then qualify for and obtain immigration visas before they may be admissible into the United States."

The *St. Louis* turned back toward Europe on June 6, 1939. About 600 of the passengers eventually died in the Holocaust.[3]

Who gets political asylum?

Between 1996 and 2005, the U.S. government accepted 60,800 refugees a year on average, and granted asylum to an average of just over 28,000 people a year.[4] Many more people apply for asylum and are rejected. If you're fleeing for your life, you may have a hard time getting hold of valid travel documents before you leave, let alone gathering proof of the harm you suffered. And if you show up at the airport or border without valid documents, or are caught trying to enter the United States without permission, you must convince an immigration officer of your credible fear of persecution, or you'll be summarily shipped back to wherever you came from, without a chance to present your case. Even if you pass the "credible fear" test, you'll likely be detained during your entire asylum process, which can take months—or years, if your case is denied and you appeal to the federal courts. From detention you'll have a hard time finding a lawyer, and collecting the evidence needed to support your case. And you'll need a lawyer; asylum rules are complex and your chances of winning on your own are minimal.

The Transactional Records Access Clearinghouse (TRAC), a nonpartisan research organization associated with Syracuse University, analyzed the 297,240 asylum cases decided by immigration judges from fiscal year 1994 through the beginning of fiscal year 2005 (the federal government's fiscal year runs from October 1 to September 30). (Slightly less than half of the people who won asylum in 2005 presented their cases "defensively," as part of removal hearings, to one of 208 special judges of the immigration court, an administrative wing of the Justice Department. The rest had their cases heard by asylum officers.) The data from October 1999 to fiscal year 2005 showed that the rate of asylum denial for applicants without lawyers was 93 percent, compared to 64 percent for those with lawyers. TRAC also documented "a significant judge-by-judge disparity," with 10 percent of judges denying asylum in 86 percent or more of their decisions, and another 10 percent denying asylum in 34 percent or fewer.[5]

There were also wide discrepancies based on country of origin. Some of these made sense: people from Burma, whose government is known for its violations of human and civil rights, had the lowest rate of denial: less than 25 percent of cases. But Russia's denial rate was also very low: 36 percent. Applicants from Colombia, which according to Human Rights Watch "presents the most serious human rights and humanitarian situation in the region"—but has a right-wing government closely allied with the United States—had a denial rate of over 64 percent. Applicants from Haiti, where in October 2005 a United Nations official called the human rights situation "catastrophic," faced a denial rate of over 83 percent.

The study included only countries with at least 100 asylum cases over the five-year period. The largest number of cases—34,093—came from China, with a denial rate of just over 53 percent. Colombia and Haiti had the next largest number of cases—13,524 and 12,675, respectively.[6]

Are all refugees treated equally?

The United States is obliged under international law to provide safe haven to people fleeing persecution. But in practice, U.S. refugee and asylum practices seem to be shaped more by the government's foreign policy objectives than by any human rights commitments.

From 1981 through 1990, during the final brutal years of the Jean-Claude "Baby Doc" Duvalier dictatorship (1971–1986) in Haiti and the subsequent interim regime, the U.S. government stopped 22,940 Haitians at sea, and allowed only 11 of them to apply for asylum. The rest were summarily returned to Haiti under a 1981 treaty signed by the Ronald Reagan and Duvalier governments. When the wave of refugees picked up again in late October 1991 after a right-wing coup deposed democratically elected president Jean-Bertrand Aristide, the United States took new steps to block the fleeing Haitians. Between November 1991 and April 1992, a U.S. military "joint task force" helped the Coast Guard intercept Haitians at sea and take them to the U.S. naval base at Guantánamo Bay, Cuba—now known worldwide as a prison where the U.S. government holds Muslims alleged to be "enemy combatants" in the "war on terror." At its most crowded, the base held more than 12,000 Haitians. Of more than 34,000 Haitians who passed through Guantánamo, 10,490 were eventually found to have a credible fear of persecution and were paroled into the United States, while the rest were sent back to Haiti. In May 1992, President George H.W. Bush ordered the Coast Guard to intercept all Haitians and immediately return them to Haiti without interviews to determine whether they were at risk of persecution.[7]

While Bill Clinton denounced the interceptions as "cruel and unjust" during his campaign, as president he maintained the policy.[8] In January 1993, the Coast Guard had a fleet of at least twenty-two ships and patrol boats encircling Haiti's coastline, along with a dozen aircraft; Aristide spokesperson Reverend Antoine Adrien called it a "floating Berlin Wall, around those seeking freedom."[9]

From 1984 to 1990, while war raged in Central America, the United States granted asylum to 25 percent of the 48,000 applicants from Nicaragua, whose leftist government the U.S. administration violently opposed. Over the same period, only 2.6 percent of the 45,000 applicants from El Salvador and 1.8 percent of the 9,500 Guatemalan applicants won asylum—the rest were dismissed as "economic migrants." At the time, both El Salvador and Guatemala had right-wing governments closely allied with the United States.

Pressure from U.S. religious and activist groups, some of which defied immigration laws by offering sanctuary in places of worship for out-of-status immigrants from Central America, eventually forced the government to loosen its restrictions. The American Baptist Churches brought a class action suit against the U.S. government on behalf of the asylum seekers, which the government finally settled in 1991 by agreeing to reopen the cases of Salvadorans and Guatemalans who had applied for and been denied asylum in the 1980s. But by then the conflicts were ending, and the United States began denying the applicants' asylum cases on the basis that their countries' circumstances had changed.[10]

In 1997, Congress passed the Nicaraguan Adjustment and Central American Relief Act (NACARA), which allowed Nicaraguans and Cubans to apply for permanent residence, and gave certain Guatemalans, Salvadorans, and nationals of the former Soviet bloc countries a chance to seek "suspension of deportation" under less restrictive pre-1996 terms. Under heavy pressure from the Haitian community, in 1998 Congress passed the Haitian Refugee Immigration Fairness Act, allowing nearly 50,000 Haitians to finally seek permanent residence under a process similar to that granted to Nicaraguans under NACARA.[11]

Why do Cubans get special treatment?

Some 800,000 Cubans immigrated to the United States between 1960 and 1980. They left Cuba for many reasons: some were opposed to the leftist revolution of 1959 and feared persecution from President Fidel Castro's communist government; wealthy and middle-class Cubans lost property or economic opportunities because of socialist policies; and poorer Cubans fled the island later as its economy stagnated, at least in part because of a U.S. embargo.

But they were able to come here because the U.S. government actively encouraged Cubans to immigrate. The government even supplied assistance to Cuban immigrants as they arrived—$1.4 billion by 1980—and in 1966 Congress passed the Cuban Adjustment Act, which allowed Cuban immigrants to apply for permanent resident status after two years in the United States, even if they entered without permission. (In 1980 the two-year wait was reduced to one year.)

Welcoming Cuban immigrants fit in with U.S. efforts in the early 1960s to bring down the Cuban government. The policy provided a pool of people who could be recruited to fight the Cuban government; at the same time, it hurt the Cuban economy by luring away academics, scientists, professionals, and experienced managers. And the streams of refugees fleeing the island hurt the reputation of the Cuban revolution.

The United States was happy to receive the first wave of Cuban immigrants, who were "disproportionately well-educated, white, and of upper-echelon occupations and income," according to New York University professor David M. Reimers. The U.S. attitude changed somewhat as Castro's government failed to collapse and as the later waves of immigrants turned out to be less "well-educated and white." After some 130,000 Cubans landed in Florida in a "freedom flotilla" from the Cuban port of Mariel in 1980, the United States restricted legal immigration from Cuba to about 20,000 people a year—the same quota as for immigrants from other countries (the limit for Cubans has risen slightly since then).[12]

But the Cuban Adjustment Act still grants automatic residency to virtually all Cubans who manage to reach U.S. shores, regardless of how they arrive and without a need to prove persecution. Under the U.S. government's "wet foot, dry foot" policy, Cubans whose "dry feet" touch U.S. soil can stay, while those caught at sea with "wet feet" are returned to Cuba. No other nationality enjoys the same privilege, and the promise of a green card encourages many Cubans to risk the journey.

4

Why Can't They Just "Get Legal"?

Is it really important who's "legal" and who's not?

"Illegality" has become one of the main cries raised by people who oppose immigration. They say they aren't against immigrants, they are just against "illegals." They try to convince us that the world is divided into two camps: good "legal" immigrants and bad "illegal" immigrants.

Being without status is not a permanent condition. People who arrive legally may fall out of status. Some who were once undocumented have become U.S. citizens. Asylum seekers who are ordered deported can win asylum in the appeals courts and eventually gain permanent residency. And immigrants who have had permanent resident status for many years have been "de-legalized," as the New York–based group Families for Freedom puts it, because of past criminal convictions, even minor ones.[1] In short, the only difference between an immigrant who is "legal" and one who is not is that one has been granted an opportunity to gain and keep legal status, while the other is still waiting for that opportunity.

Some people say it's unfair to allow "illegals" to cut ahead in line instead of "waiting their turn," and that it's an affront to the immigrants who are trying to do things the "right way." But most authorized immigrants have family members and friends who are still trying to gain legal status, and they understand how difficult it is. So it's not surprising that a majority feel sympathy for the undocumented. In a telephone survey of 800 authorized immigrants taken by Bendixen & Associates in February and March of 2006 for New America Media, 68 percent supported granting out-of-status immigrants a temporary work permit and a way to gain legal residency. (The respondents were 55 percent Latino, 30 percent Asian, and 15 percent European or African. More than half of them were naturalized U.S. citizens.)[2]

How "illegal" is immigration, anyway?

As of February 2007, entering the United States without permission from the federal government (by sneaking across the border, for example) is a criminal offense—a minor misdemeanor, with a maximum sentence of six months. Living or working here without permission from the federal government— regardless of how you entered—is just a civil infraction, not a crime. While some local officials try to claim such "illegal presence" is like trespassing, it's more comparable under the law to a ticket for jaywalking.

Some people point out that out-of-status immigrants commit a crime when they use false documents to get jobs. (Many are left with little choice if they want to work, and employers conveniently turn a blind eye.) Working for a living doesn't harm society, and most people consider it to be a good thing. But for some reason, immigrants face more public condemnation—and harsher legal consequences—for using fake IDs to get honest jobs than U.S.-born teenagers do when they use fake IDs to buy liquor.

Why are immigrants held to a higher standard than U.S. citizens? Most U.S.-born citizens have broken some laws during their lifetimes, yet no one calls them "illegals."

The vast majority of immigrants don't want to break any laws, even minor ones. If given the opportunity, they would rather come here safely and legally, with valid documents, and stay out of trouble.

Criminal or Civil?

Under the 1952 Immigration and Nationality Act (INA), the U.S. government can impose both criminal and civil penalties for violations of immigration law. Criminal charges are presented in federal court, while civil violations generally involve removal proceedings in immigration court, a separate administrative system under the Department of Justice that provides defendants with fewer due process guarantees. (In immigration proceedings, for example, you have no right to a court-appointed lawyer.)

Under INA Section 275 (8 U.S.C. 1325), "illegal entry" is a federal criminal misdemeanor with a maximum sentence of six months in jail and a fine. ("Illegal reentry"—returning to the United States without permission after being deported—is a more serious felony crime.) Unlawful presence in the United States, on the other hand—just being here out of status—is merely a violation of a civil statute and can result in deportation.[3]

With HR 4437, a bill passed by the House of Representatives on December 16, 2005, lawmakers sought to criminalize out-of-status immigrants by lumping together unlawful presence with "illegal entry," increasing the maximum sentence to a year and a day, and turning the crime into a felony. The bill sparked unprecedented mass protests—including school and job walkouts—by millions of immigrants in the spring of 2006. The Senate didn't support the House proposal, and by the end of the 2006 legislative session, most of its provisions had not become law.

Why don't immigrants "follow the rules"?

The rules are made to keep immigrants out. Most people who would like to come to the United States—temporarily or permanently—cannot get a visa to come here legally.

No one actually prefers to risk their life trudging across the desert for days without water, stuffed into sealed train cars or truck beds, stowed away in shipping containers, crawling through sewage tunnels, or floating on inner tubes across polluted rivers or shark-infested oceans. People do it because they have no safe, legal way to get here…and lots of compelling reasons to come.

Don't all immigrants bring their extended families here?

U.S. citizens can bring their "immediate relatives"—spouses, parents or children—here as permanent residents, but the rules are complicated, the bureaucracy is burdensome, and the process can often take years. For other types of "family preferences," an even more complex set of rules lays out "priority" categories and annual caps based on the family relationship and country of origin. Waiting times of ten to twenty years are not uncommon, and while they wait, applicants are disqualified from visiting the United States because they have shown "immigrant intent."

The politicians who introduced the "family preference" system into the 1965 Immigration Act billed it as a way to keep Asians and Africans out of the United States. Congress was eliminating the 1924 national-origin quotas, which had ensured that most immigrants came from Britain, Scandinavia, and Germany. Representative Emmanuel Celler, a New York Democrat who cosponsored the 1965 law, said in Congress during the final debate on the bill that family preferences would mean "there will not be, comparatively, many Asians or Africans entering the country….[S]ince the people of Africa and Asia have very few relatives here, comparatively few could immigrate from those countries because they have no family ties to the U.S."[4]

Isn't there some kind of "visa lottery"?

In 1986, Congress created a temporary category of "diversity" visas to bolster immigration from Europe, which had slowed thanks to the 1965 law and a growing European economy.[5] The Immigration Act of 1990 made the program permanent starting in 1995. The "Diversity Immigrant Visa Program," as it's officially called, allocates 50,000 immigrant visas to different parts of the world under a formula favoring regions that have sent relatively few immigrants in the previous five years. Natives of countries that have sent more than 50,000 immigrants to the United States during the past five years are disqualified from participating.[6]

Is it really so hard to get a tourist visa?

As of 2006, citizens of twenty-seven countries—all of Western Europe plus Japan, Singapore, Brunei, New Zealand, and Australia—were eligible for a "visa waiver," meaning they don't need to apply for a visa to visit the United States. In the rest of the world, U.S. visas are very difficult to get, and at least a quarter of the people who apply are rejected—often after waiting in long lines and paying hefty application fees.[7] (An even larger number of people don't bother applying, since they know they won't qualify under the restrictive rules.) Mexicans applying for U.S. visas in 2006 had to pay a $100 fee, plus an additional $85 if embassy officials decided to require a complete fingerprint check.[8] In Mexico, $185 is more than a month's salary at minimum wage.

To get a visitor visa, you have to show that you don't plan to stay in the United States. To demonstrate this, you will generally be expected to prove you have a stable job or a profitable business, close family ties in your country, several thousand dollars in the bank, and a home or other property.

But consular officers also judge visa applicants on their appearance. In the early 1990s, the U.S. consulate in São Paulo, Brazil routinely denied visas to applicants who "looked poor"—which generally meant they had darker skin—regardless of other criteria. Officers would mark applications with abbreviations such as "LP" (looks poor), "TP" (talks poor), or "LR" (looks rough), according to a lawsuit brought by a fired consular officer who objected to the discrimination. In January 1998, a U.S. federal judge ruled that the screening policies used at the consulate in São Paulo from 1992 to 1994 were "clearly illegal."[9]

Even for those whose applications are approved, "a visa does not guarantee entry into the United States," as U.S. embassy websites warned in 2006. In fact, the final decision on whether to let someone into the country is made by an immigration officer at the port of entry. You can arrive with a valid visa in hand

and still be turned away at the airport and put on the next flight home because
the immigration officer doesn't like the way you look.

"Yacht People"

The Immigration Reform Act, signed by President George H.W. Bush
on November 29, 1990, created a new category of visa for millionaire
investors. Up to 10,000 immigration visas a year were made available
under the EB-5 category to anyone investing $1 million into a U.S.
business and creating at least ten jobs for U.S. citizens. The investment can be smaller—$500,000—if made in rural or high unemploy-
ment areas. A total of 4,496 people got investor visas in the decade
from fiscal year 1996 to 2005.[10]

As Harold Ezell, former Immigration and Naturalization Service (INS)
western regional commissioner, said in 1991, "We've done a great job
on boat people. I see no problem with a few yacht people." After leaving his INS post in 1989, Ezell began marketing investor visas to
wealthy foreigners.[11] Ezell was one of a number of government officials who pushed for the investor visa program, then left for the private sector to reap profits from it, as revealed in a February 2000
Baltimore Sun exposé.[12]

Those profits were boosted when Immigration and Naturalization
Service deputy general counsel Paul Virtue issued legal opinions in
1993 and 1995 loosening the rules for the investor visas. The controversial rules were reversed in late 1997, but the scandal led the U.S.
Justice Department's Inspector General to launch an investigation in
1998 into the "appearance of impropriety" in the behavior of high-level
government employees. The investigation concluded that Virtue had
arranged special access to key agency officials for a private company,
American Immigration Services (AIS). The Inspector General's office
closed the case without taking further action in October 1999, and its
report was kept secret.[13]

Aren't there lots of other ways to come here legally?

There is a whole alphabet soup of visa categories, each with its own set of confusing and restrictive rules. Most of the people who have been displaced by economic and political crises around the world don't fit any of these categories.

To get a student visa, students must show they have strong ties in their home country and enough money to support themselves and pay their full-time tuition without working outside school. A massive database known as SEVIS (Student and Exchange Visitor Information System), mandated under the 1996 Illegal Immigration Reform and Immigrant Responsibility Act, links school records with government records, so the immigration service automatically revokes the visas of students who drop out, flunk out, or stop taking a full course load.

An "exchange visitor" visa, used for au pairs and camp counselors, also allows university students to come to the United States to work for four months at temporary jobs (such as seasonal work at ski resorts, for example). Students pay hefty fees to contracting companies to participate, and often find that the pay and working conditions are worse than what they were promised. Visa categories also exist for athletes, artists, entertainers, religious workers, "intracompany transferees," and "workers of extraordinary ability or achievement," among others.

Once immigrants have been here a while, can't they "get legal"?

Hundreds of thousands of immigrants have lived in the United States for many years without status and are eager to gain legal permanent residency. Those who have a valid option for legalizing their status generally pursue it, even though the process can be expensive and can take years. In 2005, a total of 738,302 people managed to adjust their status to permanent resident. At the end of 2005 there were still 900,000 such applications pending a decision.[14]

But there are only a few ways to "get legal," and most out-of-status immigrants don't qualify. As of 2006, people who enter the United States without permission can't even gain legal status by marrying a U.S. citizen.

Isn't there some kind of "waiver"?

For a few years there was a clause called Section 245(i), which was first added to the Immigration and Nationality Act in 1994. Often referred to as a waiver, it allowed people who came across the border "illegally" ("entered without inspection" in immigration law jargon) to pay a fine and adjust their status here, without having to return to their country and apply for a visa. Section 245(i) expired on January 14, 1998, but the Legal Immigration Family Equity Act (LIFE), signed by President Bill Clinton on December 21, 2000, brought it back temporarily, creating a brief window of opportunity for immigrants who could get their petitions filed by April 30, 2001. Thousands applied during that four-month period, creating a major backlog. (The new law also temporarily broadened the opportunities for "labor certification," the process by which employers can sponsor their employees for green cards.)[15]

Since May 2001, with 245(i) no longer on the books, people who entered the United States "without inspection" can't adjust their status here, even if they marry a U.S. citizen. Instead they must leave and apply for a visa from outside the United States. Once out of the country, they are trapped by the punitive provisions of the 1996 Illegal Immigration Reform and Immigrant Responsibility Act's Section 301. Under those provisions, anyone who has been "unlawfully present" in the United States for more than 180 days is deemed "excludable" and barred from returning for three years. Anyone with more than twelve months of "unlawful presence" is barred for ten years.

Who can "get legal"?

If you found yourself out of status after entering the United States with a valid visa, you might be able to get permanent residency (a green card) through family ties or employer sponsorship. This isn't always easy—any encounter with the immigration bureaucracy is likely to be plagued with obstacles and frustrations.

Getting an employer to sponsor you for permanent residency is especially complicated, and can often take more than five years. Employers are frequently reluctant to go along with the tax and salary requirements involved—especially since it means they have to admit they've been hiring out-of-status workers in the first place. Before your file even gets to the immigration agency, the Department of Labor must certify that your employer tried unsuccessfully to find U.S. citizens or permanent residents who could do your job.

If you have a spouse, parent, or adult child ("immediate relative" in immigration terms) who is a U.S. citizen, they can sponsor you for permanent residency. You'll have to show that you have "good moral character" and won't be a burden to the welfare system. Siblings or other relatives get lower priority under the "family preference" system and can face wait times of a decade or more.

Many people believe that getting a green card through marriage is just a matter of filling out a few forms and answering a few questions—as long as the relationship is legitimate. But the way the government looks at it, the burden is on you—the applicant—to prove your marriage isn't fraudulent. You and your spouse are expected to get a joint checking account, pay taxes jointly, and have bills and leases in both your names, among other steps (even though many other married couples don't do these things).[16] The whole process from marriage to green card generally takes one to three years, but can take longer.[17]

And if your life partner isn't of the opposite sex, you're flat out of luck. At least nineteen nations around the world—including the United Kingdom, Spain, South Africa, Israel, and Brazil—provide some form of immigration benefits to the same-sex partners of citizens and permanent residents, but the United States is not among them.[18]

What about the so-called "anchor babies"?

Under the Constitution, babies born in the United States are U.S. citizens, even if their parents are out-of-status immigrants. Opponents of immigration like to call such children "anchor babies," implying that immigrant parents use their U.S.-born children as a way to establish themselves here. But having a U.S. citizen child doesn't give immigrants a path to legal status, or protect them from deportation. U.S. citizens have to be at least twenty-one years old to sponsor their parents for legal residency. Each year, thousands of people who have U.S.-born children are deported, leaving families shattered.

Before 1996, out-of-status immigrants could sometimes win "suspension of deportation" by proving they had lived in the United States for seven years and had good moral character, and their removal would cause "extreme" hardship to themselves or to a family member with legal status. But the 1996 Illegal Immigration Reform and Immigrant Responsibility Act (IIRIRA) changed the rules. To be granted what is now called "cancellation of removal," applicants must prove they have lived here for ten years with good moral character, and their deportation would cause "exceptional and extremely unusual" hardship to a U.S. citizen or permanent resident parent, spouse, or child.[19] It's very difficult to meet the hardship criteria: a child who is separated from a parent clearly suffers hardship, but the situation is certainly not exceptional or extremely unusual. When such cancellation is granted, it usually goes to an immigrant parent who is the primary care giver for a U.S. citizen child suffering from a severe, life-threatening medical condition.

The 1996 law also set a limit of 4,000 on the number of people who can be granted this particular type of cancellation in a given year (not counting permanent residents seeking to reverse deportation orders, who are counted separately and are not subject to the cap). It is so difficult to win cancellation on the basis of "exceptional and extremely unusual hardship" that the ceiling of 4,000 has never been reached. In 2005, the immigration courts granted 3,093 of these cases.[20]

Couldn't immigrants become U.S. citizens if they wanted to?

It's a common misconception that undocumented immigrants could just become U.S. citizens if they wanted to, and if they bothered to apply. But immigrants must first become permanent residents, then wait five years before they can apply to become a naturalized citizen. (If you are married to a U.S. citizen, you can apply for citizenship three years after getting your green card; U.S. soldiers on active duty can take advantage of a more accelerated schedule.)

Some permanent residents hesitate to go through the naturalization process because it seems expensive or too much of a bureaucratic hassle.

Others don't apply because their home country doesn't allow dual citizenship, and they may lose certain rights there by becoming U.S. citizens. Some permanent legal residents are barred from gaining citizenship because of prior criminal convictions.

For those who do seek citizenship, the process is not always straightforward. If you are married to a U.S. citizen, immigration agents may question your marriage again. If you travel outside the United States for more than a few months each year, your application can be denied (and they may even try to take your green card away). Any past arrests will resurface through fingerprint records checks, and may get you deported. Even if your record is clean, you may be confused with someone with a similar name and prior arrests. In one such case, a permanent resident from Peru who had never even received as much as a parking ticket was denied citizenship based on crimes committed by someone with the same first and last name and the same birth date—even though the person who committed the crimes was born in the United States, was a foot taller, and had a different middle name. While such confusions would be easy to clear up quickly through fingerprint comparisons, immigration officials refused to fix the mistake and grant citizenship until a lawyer sued them in federal court.[21]

Citizenship applicants may also face unexplained delays. "Despite serving in the U.S. Air Force, I have been waiting for my citizenship for more than two years," said California resident Mustafa Aziz, who was only a year old when he and his family escaped war-torn Afghanistan and moved to the United States. The government left Aziz waiting for his citizenship while it allegedly carried out a type of background check known as a "name check." In August 2006, with the "name check" still dragging on and no end in sight, Aziz and nine others in similar situations sued the government with help from the American Civil Liberties Union (ACLU) of Southern California, the ACLU Immigrants' Rights Project, and the Council on American-Islamic Relations (CAIR). In October 2006, two months after the suit was filed, the government announced it would finally grant citizenship to Aziz and six of the other plaintiffs. The lawsuit is seeking to get the immigration service to start following set deadlines on its "name checks."[22]

5

Is It Easy to Be "Illegal"?

Is it easy to live here "illegally"?

Living in the United States without valid immigration status was never easy, but it has become extremely difficult over the past decade as politicians have enacted a multitude of anti-immigrant laws at the federal, state, and local level. In most states, laws block out-of-status immigrants from seeking drivers licenses. Immigrants who lack documents may have trouble finding a place to live, opening a bank account, applying for jobs, registering for school, or getting medical treatment. They must often avoid traveling, since buses, trains, and even private cars may be stopped by officers checking immigration documents.

Such restrictions force many out-of-status immigrants into situations that are sometimes risky (such as keeping their savings in cash, and avoiding hospitals) or illegal (driving without a license). As they become more vulnerable, out-of-status immigrants are more likely to be exploited by unscrupulous employers, landlords, immigration law "consultants," and others who try to take advantage of them, knowing they will be hesitant to report the abuse.

Immigration raids set off a wave of terror in communities; people are afraid to venture into the streets, even to shop for food or take their children to school. The kids who do make it to class spend the day worrying that their parents may be arrested at work. When immigration agents arrested 1,200 workers across the country in a single day as part of an investigation into the pallet company IFCO Systems in April 2006, the sweep sparked what Florida Immigrant Advocacy Center director Cheryl Little called "the worst climate of fear...in more than two decades."

"People are scared to even go in the streets now, fearing they are going to be picked up, questioned," said Dennis D. Grant, the Jamaican-American senior pastor of Restoration Ministries in Margate and Miramar, Florida. "They are in a state of panic right now."[1]

Even some immigrants with permanent legal residence are now at risk because a past arrest or conviction makes them eligible for deportation under retroactive laws passed in 1996. They too are trapped, unable to travel, and live with the daily fear of being detained and deported.

That same fear affects out-of-status immigrants who are victims of crime. While it's hard to measure without firm statistics, anecdotal evidence suggests that in many areas, undocumented immigrants have become a favorite target of robbers, who take advantage of the fact that their victims are often paid in cash and are too afraid of deportation to report the crimes to the police.[2] Immigrant victims of domestic violence, too, have a low rate of seeking help from authorities. A survey conducted by the Washington, D.C.-based nonprofit immigrant service agency Ayuda in 1993 noted that 83 percent of the battered immigrants interviewed did not contact law enforcement agencies about their abuse. One-fifth of the women surveyed reported that abusive partners had threatened them with deportation or refusal to file immigration papers.[3]

Immigrants are also targeted in hate crimes—for example, in Farmingville, Long Island (New York), where in 2000 two white men carried out a premeditated racist attack against two undocumented Mexican day laborers, beating them nearly to death. Because of the violence of the assault, and the publicity that accompanied it, the undocumented victims actually won justice: their attackers were sentenced to twenty-five years in prison for attempted murder.[4] But most hate crimes go unreported and unsolved. (Since September 11, 2001, immigrants who are perceived as Muslim, Middle Eastern, or South Asian have been especially targeted.)[5]

Undocumented immigrants are often separated from their families for years, even decades. Their lack of status means they are stuck in the United States, and they can't visit family or friends back home without losing everything they have built here. (Mexican immigrants in the United States used to visit Mexico more often, but increased enforcement has made the journey so dangerous and costly that most no longer risk it.)[6] Even those immigrants who have some of their family members here have been forced to leave other loved ones behind. Many immigrants come from close extended families, making the separation especially painful.

What leads someone to make such a harsh choice? Often, it's the love they feel for their families that leads people to migrate. "Our situation doesn't give us the luxury to live together and live well; it can't be done," Mexican immigrant Ramón Castillo explained to filmmaker Heather Courtney in the 2001 documentary *Los Trabajadores* (The Workers). Unable to make ends meet in Mexico, Castillo left his wife and two daughters behind to find work in Austin, Texas. He sent most of the money he earned back home to pay for his daughters' schooling, in the hopes that they could become professionals and have a better future. "You either live well, or you live together. If you live together, you don't live well, because there isn't enough to live on. If you live well, you need to leave your family to make good money, so they can live well."[7]

Immigrants who remain here for years without status often feel condemned to an underground existence in the "cage of gold," as the song "Jaula de Oro" by the popular Mexican band Los Tigres del Norte explains:

What use is money
If I'm like a prisoner
Within this great nation?
When I remember it makes me cry
The cage may be made of gold
But it doesn't stop being a prison.[8]

Do immigrants have the right to an education?

All immigrant children, regardless of their status, have the right to public education through the high-school level. The Supreme Court upheld this principle in the June 1982 *Plyler v. Doe* decision, which overturned a Texas state law denying school funding for undocumented students.

The situation is more complicated when it comes to higher education like college, university, or technical schools. While many countries consider such education to be a universal right, the United States generally treats it as a privilege. Still, many community colleges and public universities in the United States provide accessible degree programs to city or state residents. In the past, it didn't matter if those students were immigrants living here without permission from the federal government.

But Section 505 of the 1996 Illegal Immigrant Reform and Immigrant Responsibility Act barred states from granting reduced tuition to undocumented state residents unless non-resident U.S. citizens in the same circumstances get the same privilege. As of April 2006, ten states had passed laws allowing undocumented students to get in-state tuition if they attended high school in the state for a certain number of years and graduated. (These state laws comply with the 1996 act by allowing U.S. citizens who meet the same state high school attendance and graduation requirements to get the same tuition rate, even if they no longer live in the state.)

As of April 2006, only about 5 to 10 percent of undocumented young people who graduate from high school go on to college, compared with about 75 percent of their classmates.[9] There are many thousands of immigrants who came here as young children, have been educated in U.S. public schools, speak perfect English, feel as "American" as anyone else, and yet still lack legal status. Now they find themselves without a future. Denied in-state tuition, unable to qualify for financial aid under federal rules, and unable to work legally, they get stuck in low-paying jobs and shut out of more promising opportunities.

Each year, an estimated 65,000 out-of-status immigrants graduate from U.S. high schools and put their dreams on hold while they watch their classmates go off to college. Angela Perez, a Colombian immigrant, didn't even apply to college despite ranking fourth in her graduating class with a 3.8 grade-point average. "It feels awful," Angela wrote in an essay during her sophomore year. "I feel frustrated. I try hard until I accomplish something and I do not want all my accomplishments to be a waste of time. I want them to be valuable. I want to be able to pay my parents back after all their support and the difficulties they have lived in order to bring me here."[10] Out-of-status students who do manage to get through college still can't pursue a career without legal status—like Kathy, another young immigrant, who graduated from Nyack College in New York with a degree in social work, but could only get a job as a nanny. "Graduation was the most depressing day of my life," she said.[11]

Are undocumented workers more exploited?

Their lack of status forces many undocumented workers into jobs where they earn less money and face more dangerous conditions than other workers. Not wanting to draw attention to their situation, and afraid of losing the jobs they have, undocumented workers are often reluctant to fight for better wages or working conditions. When out-of-status immigrants do try to defend their workplace rights—and many do—they face an uneven playing field. Employers may suddenly decide to fire workers who lack documents, or use the threat of raids and deportation to squelch organizing efforts.

Out-of-status men who worked in Los Angeles County's huge informal economy made an average of $16,553 a year in 2004, according to a study by the Economic Roundtable, a nonprofit research organization. Out-of-status women averaged just $7,630. Although they worked in major industries like apparel and textile manufacturing, these workers were paid far below industry standards, and much less than the $24,800-a-year average wage for male citizens who didn't finish high school.[12]

Greg Beeman, president of the Massachusetts Chapter of Associated Builders and Contractors, explained that construction industry bosses often exploit undocumented workers by classifying employees as independent contractors, paying cash that is not reported as income, paying workers no overtime, paying wage rates barely half the industry standards, and violating child-labor laws.[13]

Undocumented workers have a far higher rate of fatal injuries on the job than other workers. Fatal workplace accidents jumped 72 percent for Latinos between 1992 and 2005, while the rate for other workers dropped 16 percent; by 2005 the fatality rate for Latinos was the highest for any group of workers, at 4.9 per 100,000 workers. While many Latinos are not immigrants, a special report in the *Chicago Tribune* concluded that the victims were largely undocumented immigrants.[14] The deaths of immigrant workers are less likely to be investigated, especially if they are undocumented. According to an in-depth 2001 report in the Long Island daily *Newsday*, the government's Occupational Safety and Health Administration (OSHA) failed to investigate 874 of the estimated 4,200 job-related deaths of immigrant workers between 1994 and 1999.[15]

Doctors and others who work with injured migrants say nonfatal workplace accidents are underreported, since out-of-status workers are afraid of losing their jobs or being deported. Dr. Eileen Couture, head of clinical care at Oak Forest Hospital in Cook County, Illinois, told the *Chicago Tribune*: "You say this [accident] has to be reported and they say, 'You don't understand, I need my job. You don't understand, I have to feed my family.' "[16]

Even when they do report an injury, out-of-status workers can't count on getting help. Francisco Ruiz, an undocumented Mexican, was injured in Charlotte, North Carolina, when a crane hoisting him collapsed; the injury left him unable to work. His employer's insurance company refused to pay any compensation beyond his initial medical bills and fought him in court for six years on the grounds that he was "illegal." His case drew attention because he was one of the few undocumented workers who managed to fight back and win.[17]

Are all workers protected by labor laws?

Under existing federal and state laws, as the courts have generally interpreted them, all workers—including immigrants—have certain rights, whether or not they are in the country legally and whether or not they have the federal government's permission to work here.

All workers have the right to be paid minimum wage for the hours they have worked, plus overtime if they work more than forty hours a week. All workers have a right to be free from discrimination in the workplace, including discrimination on the basis of race, religion, national origin, language, or accent (although undocumented workers who file discrimination claims will not generally be able to win reinstatement in their jobs).[18] All workers have a right to a healthy and safe workplace, and those who are injured on the job have a right to compensation. All workers have the right to join a union, or to organize themselves in defense of their common interests.

These rights are often violated. But although they face obstacles, many undocumented workers have successfully defended their rights through the courts, or through grassroots public pressure campaigns, with the help of workplace justice advocates.

In March 2002, the Supreme Court ruled in *Hoffman Plastic Compounds, Inc. v. NLRB* that while it's illegal for an employer to fire an undocumented worker in retaliation for trying to organize a union, such employees are *not* entitled to compensation for wages they would have earned if they had been able to keep working. By contrast, the courts have generally upheld the right of workers—regardless of their immigration status—to be paid for hours they actually worked, since to rule otherwise would be to endorse slavery. Courts have generally also defended the right to compensation in cases of discrimination or workplace injury. A number of judges have noted that it is unfair—and harmful to all workers—to allow employers to exploit undocumented workers and then escape their responsibilities in court by arguing that the workers' lack of immigration status means they have no right to compensation.[19]

In June 2002, U.S. district judge Whitman Knapp of the Southern District of New York ruled that clothing manufacturer Donna Karan International Inc. was not entitled to learn the immigration status of a group of workers who were charging the company with maintaining sweatshop conditions. Knapp said the possibility that the information would be used to intimidate plaintiffs outweighed its relevance to the case.[20]

In a September 2002 case in Illinois, *Rodriguez v. The Texan*, a federal judge noted: "[I]t surely comes with ill grace for an employer to hire alien workers and

then, if the employer itself proceeds to violate the Fair Labor Standards
Act...for it to try to squirm out of its own liability on such grounds."[21]

The U.S. Equal Employment Opportunity Commission (EEOC) confirmed in June 2002 that it won't inquire into the immigration status of workers
claiming discrimination, and won't consider such status when investigating
cases. Referring specifically to the Hoffman case, EEOC Commissioner Leslie
E. Silverman insisted in a press release: "[M]ake no mistake, it is still illegal for
employers to discriminate against undocumented workers."[22]

Do immigrants have constitutional rights?

The Bill of Rights (the first ten amendments to the Constitution, ratified in
1791) refers to the rights of "people," not citizens. The First Amendment
specifically guarantees freedom of speech and of religion, and "the right of the
people peaceably to assemble, and to petition the Government for a redress of
grievances." Under the Bill of Rights, freedom from "unreasonable searches
and seizures," from deprivation "of life, liberty, or property, without due
process of law," from "excessive bail," "excessive fines," and "cruel and unusual
punishments" are among the rights guaranteed to all persons—not only to the
citizens of the United States. The Sixth Amendment guarantees any defendant
in a criminal case—not only citizens—the right to a speedy public trial by jury
with the assistance of a lawyer. Article One, Section 9 of the U.S. Constitution,
indicates that anyone can use the writ of habeas corpus to go before a judge to
challenge his or her imprisonment.

From the beginning, all these and other rights were systematically and
openly denied to African Americans. Slavery remained legal and continued to
exist for another seventy-four years after the Bill of Rights was ratified. The
Supreme Court declared in the Dred Scott case of March 1857 that people of
African descent—whether slave or free—did not have an inherent right to U.S.
citizenship. Because it defended this injustice so blatantly, the Dred Scott ruling actually fueled the movement against slavery. In December 1865, the
Thirteenth Amendment was ratified, banning slavery, and in July 1868, the
Fourteenth Amendment was ratified, stating:

All persons born or naturalized in the United States, and subject to the jurisdiction thereof, are citizens of the United States and of the State wherein they reside. No State shall make or enforce any law which shall abridge the privileges or immunities of citizens of the United States; nor shall any State deprive any person of life, liberty, or property, without due process of law; nor deny to any person within its jurisdiction the equal protection of the laws.

Even here, where citizenship rights are defined, the last two clauses very clearly refer not to citizens but to "any person" and "any person within [a state's] jurisdiction." This language clearly extends due process rights and equal protection to immigrants, regardless of their legal status. (Some people have suggested amending the Constitution to eliminate the automatic "birthright citizenship" guaranteed by the Fourteenth Amendment, so that children born in the United States to out-of-status immigrants would not be U.S. citizens. This would be extremely unfair—children don't get to choose where they are born, and many would end up being stateless under such a system.)

The Dred Scott case is a reminder that even when the Supreme Court upholds discriminatory policies as the "law of the land," we can fight back and eventually win policy changes that reflect the values of freedom, justice, and equal rights. Court decisions don't happen in a vacuum; if the people move, the courts will follow. As Riva Enteen, program director of the National Lawyers Guild's San Francisco chapter, put it in a 2002 interview: "[I]t takes a political movement to create a political context in which the courts respond and, frankly, do the right thing. So, if there wasn't a civil rights movement, the Supreme Court would not have [made its 1954 ruling in the] *Brown v. Board [of Education* case] to integrate the schools."[23]

Today, equality under the law exists on paper for African Americans and other citizens of color—although in practice, pervasive discrimination means their rights are often violated with impunity. Non-citizens, by contrast, don't even have true equality on paper. The way the courts have interpreted the laws and the Constitution, immigrants don't have the *right* to be here in the first place—even if you're a legal permanent resident, your presence here is generally considered a *privilege*. Through this twist of logic, the government claims it can deport any non-citizen for virtually any reason, or for no reason at all—even longtime residents with green cards. This means non-citizens end up being denied a number of rights that should be guaranteed to "all persons"—like free speech, or freedom from unjust imprisonment, and from cruel and unusual punishment. If you are a non-citizen, you can be deported for exercising your freedom of expression, imprisoned without being charged with a crime, or exiled for life from the country you consider your home.

Do immigrants have the right to protest?

The First Amendment guarantees that everyone—immigrants as well as U.S.-born citizens—has the right to take part in public protests. Some people feel angry or resentful when they see immigrants exercising these rights, as when thousands marched and rallied across the United States between March and May of 2006 to defend immigrant rights. There seems to be an unspoken but widely held belief that out-of-status immigrants should stay "in their place" as silent cogs in the labor machine—hardworking, quiet, fearful, and out of sight. During the civil rights movement of the 1960s, African Americans who rose up against segregation and oppression saw similar reactions from whites—even among those who supported their rights but thought they should wait patiently for them rather than march.

But rights don't come to those who wait. "Power concedes nothing without a demand. It never did and it never will," noted prominent African-American writer, orator, and anti-slavery activist Frederick Douglass in a speech in August 1857, a few months after the Dred Scott decision.

How can you tell who's a citizen and who's not?

The United States has no national ID card for its citizens, because so many people see national ID cards as an infringement of privacy rights and civil liberties. This means there is no easy way for the authorities—or anyone else—to figure out who's a U.S. citizen and who's not.

People who came here from other countries (even if they have become U.S. citizens) can be required to show documents proving they are in the United States legally. But how can anyone distinguish a native-born U.S. citizen from an immigrant? We can't tell by physical appearance or accent, since native-born citizens have diverse ethnic and linguistic backgrounds, just as immigrants do.

In reality, law enforcement officers make judgments about whether someone is an immigrant based on their own prejudices. But it's not actually legal to question people just because of the way they look or talk. In July 2005, an immigration judge in Arizona halted the deportation of four high school students arrested during a school trip to Niagara Falls, ruling that Border Patrol agents had illegally singled them out for questioning on the basis of their appearance. The four students were from Mexico, but had lived in the United States since they were children.[24]

6

Are Immigrants Hurting Our Economy?

How much do immigrants cost us?

When they first come to the United States, some immigrants may get more out of the system than they put in. This is because they tend to be younger than the population as a whole; like most younger working people, they make less money and pay less taxes at the same time that they are raising children—most of them U.S.-born citizens—who go to school and benefit from public health services.

The National Academy of Sciences calculated in 1997 that households headed by immigrants were costing households headed by native-born citizens some $166 to $226 a year, mostly in public education and health expenses for children. The number was even higher for states with large immigrant populations: in California, the cost was $1,178 for households headed by native-born citizens.

Taken out of context, this number seems like ammunition for immigration opponents. But native-born young people with families are also a "burden" on the system in exactly the same way—they too make less money and pay less in taxes when they're raising their children. Both immigrants and the native born usually end up paying more into the system than they take out once they're older and their children have finished school and left home. The National

Academy of Sciences study concluded that in the long run, immigrants and their children more than make up for what they may get at the beginning.[1]

Do immigrants collect welfare?

The United States doesn't exactly have a generous welfare state—compared to Western European countries, for example—and the vast majority of immigrants come here for jobs, not handouts. In any case, few out-of-status immigrants risk applying for benefits they aren't legally entitled to, and even authorized migrants have been cut off from most public assistance.

"The United States welfare system is rapidly becoming a deluxe retirement home for the elderly of other countries," Robert Rector of the conservative Heritage Foundation complained to a congressional subcommittee in 1996.[2] Later that year, Congress passed and President Bill Clinton signed the Personal Responsibility and Work Opportunity Reconciliation Act, which drastically reduced public assistance for lawful permanent residents who entered the United States after August 1996.

The law cut permanent residents off from food stamps and Supplemental Security Income (SSI), which provides assistance to the aged, blind, and disabled, and allowed them to be barred from Temporary Assistance for Needy Families (TANF) and Medicaid until they have lived in the country for five years. Since 1996 Congress has softened some of the measures, but the effects are still drastic. From 1994 to 1998, legal permanent residents' use of TANF benefits fell by 60 percent, food stamps by 48 percent, Social Security insurance by 32 percent, and Medicaid by 15 percent. Access to food stamps was restored in 2002.[3]

Do immigrants pay taxes?

Some 71 percent of immigrants are naturalized citizens or legal residents, and pay all the same taxes as U.S.-born citizens. The other 29 percent of immigrants—those who lack legal status—mostly pay the same taxes, too. Everyone pays local sales taxes, and contributes to property taxes when buying or renting a place to live (landlords factor property taxes into the rents they charge).

About 75 percent of this country's 7.2 million out-of-status workers are employed in the formal economy—that is, they are working on the books.[4] Many of these workers are forced to use false documents, often including fake Social Security numbers, to get jobs, and most have taxes deducted from their paychecks. In fact, these workers probably pay more in taxes than U.S. citizens and authorized migrants, since they are less likely to claim any refunds they might be owed.

Out-of-status workers and their employers also pay an estimated $6 billion to $7 billion in Social Security taxes each year and about $1.5 billion in Medicaid taxes. This amount accounts for about 10 percent of Social Security's annual surplus. Very few of these workers are able to get back what they paid in. Most never expect to apply, but if they did, they would be barred by the Social Security Protection Act of 2004. This law in effect confiscates these workers' benefits because they worked here without authorization.[5]

The other 25 percent of undocumented workers—about 1.8 million—work off the books. Their employers don't report their income, and their income taxes aren't deducted from their pay. So how much revenue are the U.S. and state governments losing because of these immigrants? Badly paid and often supporting deductible dependents, the average undocumented worker in the informal economy probably owes $1,500 a year or less in federal income tax; the total tax loss for the federal government would be less than $2.7 billion annually.[6] By comparison, as many as 25 million U.S. citizens earn a large part of their income from the informal economy; the Internal Revenue Service (IRS) has estimated that the federal government loses $195 billion a year in revenue from the informal economy.[7]

How much do out-of-status immigrants get back?

Whether or not they pay income taxes, out-of-status adults generally can't get welfare or other social services beyond emergency medical care. The 1996 "welfare reform" law specifically barred states from giving any federal welfare benefits to immigrants who lack status.[8] (Some out-of-status immigrants do seek benefits for their U.S.-born children, who are entitled to the same services as other U.S. citizens.)

Out-of-status immigrant children are entitled to free public education in the United States. In fact, education is mandatory—all school-age children must attend classes, and get required vaccinations (provided by public health services). Public education and vaccination programs benefit everyone by maintaining the skill levels necessary for a modern society and preventing the spread of contagious diseases. In any case, these services are largely covered by local sales and property taxes, which everyone pays.

Opponents of immigration often claim undocumented immigrants strain health services, especially in border states like Texas, by overusing hospital emergency rooms, where federal law requires that everyone must be treated. But a survey of 46,000 people in sixty communities found that the highest emergency room usage was in Cleveland and Boston, cities with relatively low percentages of uninsured patients and immigrants from Latin America. Administrators at Dallas and Fort Worth hospitals told the *New York Times* that most of their immigrant patients have jobs, pay taxes, and have a better record of paying their bills than low-income citizens do.[9]

The 9/11 Victims

The vast majority of unauthorized immigrants are too wary of detection to file for any government benefits—even when they are clearly entitled to them.

At least forty undocumented workers are known to have been killed in the September 11, 2001, attack on New York's World Trade Center, and the number is likely higher.[10] Five years later, only eleven survivors of these workers were receiving benefits from the federal government under the September 11th Victim Compensation Fund. The fund's rules specified that undocumented immigrants were eligible for the compensation and that immigration authorities wouldn't use the information to track them down. But the survivors were still reluctant to apply, and at least one widow had to be convinced by a lawyer that it would be safe—even though the benefits range from $875,000 to $4.1 million. One survivor, a widower, refused to apply because he didn't want "charity"; he finally decided to apply when his lawyer told him the money would help his preschool-age daughter. "It's all for her," he told a reporter. "That she becomes a doctor, a lawyer. That she's not the same as me."[11]

Do remittances drain the economy?

Immigrants in the United States tend to send large amounts of the money they make to relatives back home. Latin American immigrants sent an estimated $28 billion home in these remittances in 2002. Mexico received $9.92 billion, mostly from the United States, in 2001; the Dominican Republic, El Salvador and Colombia each got between $1.5 billion and $2 billion. These payments are a huge part of the economies of poorer countries—remittances made up 24.2 percent of Haiti's gross domestic product (GDP) in 2001, for example.[12]

Big as they are, these payments aren't big enough to have a major impact on the total U.S. economy, and most go to countries like Mexico which are tightly linked to the United States economically—so that a lot of the money comes back in purchases of U.S. goods and services.

U.S. politicians and corporations generally don't complain about the remittances. In 2002, immigrants paid about $4 billion in fees for sending remittances to Latin America and the Caribbean; most of this went to U.S. banks or to U.S. corporations like Western Union.[13] Washington, for its part, uses the remittances as a hidden form of foreign aid for friendly governments—letting Central American immigrants, for example, stay in the United States to help bolster pro-U.S. governments in the region with the dollars they send home.

Do immigrants take our jobs?

This is one of the few immigration questions that most economists can agree on. In 1994 the conservative Alexis de Tocqueville Institution concluded that the "evidence suggests that immigrants create at least as many jobs as they take, and that their presence should not be feared by U.S. workers."[14] Twelve years later the liberal Pew Hispanic Center came to a similar conclusion based on a study of employment trends in the 1990s and the early 2000s.[15]

Immigrants take jobs, but they also buy goods and services, creating more jobs. In fact, immigrants probably generate more jobs than many older residents: immigrants are younger and more likely to have children at home, so they spend much more of their income on goods like clothes and food, which involve labor-intensive production. Older and richer people are much more likely to put their money into luxuries and speculative investments, which generate relatively few jobs.

Don't they just take jobs we don't want?

The fact that immigrants create as many jobs as they take doesn't mean that immigrants don't compete with native-born workers for specific jobs, or that employers don't replace native-born workers with immigrants who accept lower wages.

Employers—and some immigrant rights advocates—argue that immigrants generally get the jobs the native born won't do. James S. Holt, an economist for a management labor law firm, took that position in testimony to Congress in 1995. Agricultural jobs "entail physical labor under adverse environmental conditions of heat, cold, sun, rain, etc.," he said. "It is work that many Americans would be physically incapable of doing on a sustained basis, and that most of the rest would prefer not to do if there are better alternatives available."[16]

In reality, the jobs done by immigrants, including out-of-status immigrants, are jobs that native-born workers have traditionally done and continue to do. The native born remain a majority in these occupations, which include construction, food manufacturing, food services, and textiles. Workers without papers made up 12–14 percent of the workforce in these areas in 2005. Unauthorized workers were 36 percent of all insulation workers and 29 percent of all roofers and drywall installers. About 21 percent of private household workers were undocumented.[17]

According to the conservative economist George Borjas, himself an immigrant to the United States from Cuba, the reason that employers prefer immigrants for these jobs is probably just that immigrants will work for less money. There is no evidence, he says, "that natives would refuse to work in these jobs if the immigrants had never arrived and employers were forced to raise wages to fill the position." Immigrants "take jobs that natives do not want *at the going wage*."[18]

Do immigrants bring down wages?

Some economists say that immigrants create a strong downward pressure on wages, while a few think that by stimulating the economy immigrants actually raise wages. Most believe that immigrant workers bring down wages for some workers, but not dramatically.

The consensus position seems to be close to estimates the National Academy of Sciences gave in 1997. According to the Academy's study, the increase in low-wage immigrant workers in the 1980s may have cut pay by 1–2 percent for "all competing native-born workers"—that is, people looking for the jobs that immigrants take, ones that generally don't require a strong command of English or a high level of formal education. The effect was strongest on the 10 percent of U.S. workers who had dropped out of high school: competition from immigrant workers may have lowered their wages by about 5 percent between 1980 and 1994.[19]

Although these numbers are fairly small in terms of the U.S. workforce, they are a serious matter for working people who are trying to survive on a low income. Five percent of the $24,800 a male high school dropout made on average in 2006[20] comes to $1,240, a real hardship for a family struggling to get by. Many of the people affected are African Americans or U.S.-born Latinos.

The downward pressure on wages doesn't just affect the lowest-paid workers. In California's San Diego County—with one of the nation's largest pool of undocumented workers, plus commuters from nearby Tijuana, Mexico—production workers averaged $28,930 a year as of May 2005, 3.2 percent below the national average of $29,890. Transportation workers made $27,070, 6 percent below the national average of $28,820.[21]

Why do they work for less?

To the extent that immigrants actually do bring down other workers' wages, it is largely because they themselves get paid less—and this then forces native-born workers in the same occupations to accept lower wages in order to compete.

Some immigrants earn less because their English is weak, or because they lack the formal education or work experience required for better-paying jobs. Another reason is simple supply and demand: as the pool of available workers grows, the price of their labor goes down. And many immigrants accept lower wages when they first come to the United States because they are used to receiving still lower wages in their home countries—although this effect diminishes as people stay and adjust to U.S. prices.

But it's only *out-of-status* immigrants who earn significantly less on average than their U.S.-born counterparts—suggesting that their lack of status is largely what accounts for the wage gap. With no access to a social safety net when they're out of work, undocumented immigrants can't be too selective about the jobs they take. If they complain about low wages or unacceptable working conditions, employers may threaten to turn them in to immigration authorities. Fear of deportation keeps these workers from reporting safety violations to government agencies, even when they are injured on the job. Their lack of status makes them a vulnerable underclass of workers that employers can exploit with near impunity.

Who benefits from low wages for immigrants?

A new wave of immigration has coincided with a stagnation of real wages for most U.S. workers. After rising 81 percent from 1947 to 1973, real wages fell 3 percent from 1973 to 1980 and have barely moved upward since then. This was despite dramatic increases in worker productivity—16.6 percent from 2000 to 2005, for example. At the same time, the country's richest 1 percent were benefiting from equally dramatic increases in their real income—by 135 percent between 1980 and 2004.[22]

There are a number of factors behind the wage stagnation, including Congress's failure to raise the minimum wage after 1996, and government policies that reduce the ability of unions to organize. But certainly a large part of the explanation is the major shift in the U.S. economy that has resulted in many jobs going to low-paid, vulnerable workers: undocumented immigrants, people thrown out of the welfare system by the 1996 welfare law, and the several million workers employed in assembly plants in Asia, Latin America, and the Caribbean producing goods for U.S. firms to sell in the United States.

All of these workers are being forced into what labor organizers call "the race to the bottom"—they must accept wretched wages and working conditions, or they will lose their jobs to other workers who are willing to accept even less. And as wages stagnate or decline, the wealthiest individuals and corporations profit.

What can we do about the "race to the bottom"?

When U.S. citizens and authorized immigrants feel their economic pay is being threatened by undocumented workers, their first reaction is often to call for more enforcement of immigration laws. But a more logical step is to try to improve pay for unauthorized workers so their low wages no longer exert downward pressure on wages in general.

For one thing, this means supporting a full legalization for the twelve million out-of-status immigrants already in the country, and ensuring that they can exercise their full labor rights.

Anti-immigrant forces denounce legalization policies like the 1986 amnesty, which allowed more than 2.5 million immigrants to adjust their status. But all workers would benefit from the increase in real wages that would likely accompany an amnesty. According to the U.S. Department of Labor, within five years of the 1986 amnesty, real wages of the newly legal workers rose an average of 15 percent. If this happened now, with 7.2 million undocumented workers, there would be a strong upward pressure on wages for other workers in the same occupations. Wages would be likely to rise for all workers in the jobs with high concentrations of undocumented immigrants, according to a University of California-Los Angeles study from 2001: by about 5 percent in agriculture, 2.75 percent in services, and 2.5 percent in manufacturing.[23]

At the same time, more of the newly authorized immigrants would work on the books and pay income taxes. As they earn higher wages, they would pay more taxes, be less reliant on public services like emergency rooms, and buy more products and services, generating economic growth. And when they fight for improved wages and job conditions, and for better services for their communities, they would have a better chance of winning.

Despite adverse conditions, out-of-status workers have already led a number of successful organizing drives, often with the support of consumer boycotts and other community activism. The AFL-CIO grasped the importance of these efforts and in 1999 reversed its position on immigration; the labor federation and most of its affiliates now back some form of legalization and encourage out-of-status immigrants to organize themselves and join unions.

Retired University of California, Berkeley professor Carlos Muñoz expects immigrant workers to revitalize labor organizing in the United States as they "get forced into activity because of their situation. Many immigrants already have a heritage of participation in movements of workers in the countries they come from....Immigrants will change us more than we'll change them."[24]

7

Is Immigration Bad for Our Health, Environment, or Culture?

Do immigrants endanger public health?

The myth that immigrants endanger public health is mostly based on the idea that dangerous infectious diseases are brought here by immigrants from impoverished "third world" countries. In fact, the main threats to life and health in the United States—heart disease, cancer, injuries, and diabetes, to name a few—aren't communicable diseases, and their root causes are right here at home.

As for the kind of diseases that we may associate with poorer countries, immigrants aren't any more likely to bring them here than are U.S. citizens who travel abroad and return. (U.S. authorities don't routinely screen people for diseases as they arrive in this country; medical exams are only required for immigrants when they seek resident status here.) Insects, birds, and other animals can also carry diseases across borders.

Some people might believe immigrants from poor countries pose more of a health risk because their countries don't provide adequate medical care. But if that's a concern, why do we let U.S.-dominated institutions like the International Monetary Fund (IMF) force so many countries to shrink their public health programs?[1]Doesn't it make more sense to encourage improved health care programs worldwide?

The United States doesn't even provide adequate health care at home. According to government data for 2004, there are approximately 46 million people—15.7 percent of the U.S. population—without any health insurance. Some may be immigrants, but many are U.S.-born workers—especially young people—whose employers don't pay health care costs, and who earn too much to qualify for Medicaid, but not enough to pay for insurance (as of 2005 the average insurance premium was over $4,000 a year, per person).[2] Out-of-status immigrants are less likely to be insured; in a study based on data from Los Angeles residents in 2000, researchers estimated that slightly fewer than 22 percent of undocumented immigrants had health insurance.[3]

Measures instituted or proposed in recent years that restrict or deny preventive health and prenatal services to undocumented immigrants, or force hospitals to ask patients for immigration documents, only make the problem worse by discouraging people from seeking timely medical attention. This ends up costing everyone more, since later treatment is less effective, riskier, and more expensive. From a public health perspective, the only rational solution is to ensure that everyone—regardless of their ability to pay or their immigration status—has access to quality preventive care and prompt medical treatment.

What about epidemics like TB and AIDS?

The website of the U.S. government's Centers for Disease Control and Prevention lists eight "communicable diseases of public health significance": HIV/AIDS, tuberculosis (TB), leprosy (also known as Hansen's Disease), and five curable venereal diseases.[4]

Immigrants account for nearly all the detected cases of leprosy in the United States. But fears of an epidemic are unfounded: leprosy has been on the decline since the 1980s; in any case, it is fully curable with antibiotics, and is spread only through very close and prolonged physical contact with an infected person who has not yet received treatment.[5]

Tuberculosis, a respiratory disease, is common in Latin America, the Caribbean, Africa, Asia, Eastern Europe, and Russia, so some people blame immigrants from those regions for bringing TB to the United States, and immigration authorities require immigrants to get tested for TB (and HIV) when they apply for refugee status or permanent residency. But while the foreign-born population in the United States increased by 61.6 percent between 1993 and 2005, the number of TB cases in this country declined steadily over the same period; as of 2005 the total number of cases was the lowest since national reporting began in 1953. Cases of multi-drug-resistant TB—which is harder to treat—have increased, especially among the foreign-born, but the numbers are very low: only 128 cases were reported nationwide in 2004.[6]

It makes even less sense to blame immigrants for tuberculosis when you consider that the tuberculosis bacterium is spread through the air in confined spaces, and contagion can largely be prevented with adequate ventilation. Yet a 1992 U.S. survey of 729 health care facilities showed that 26 percent of isolation rooms and 89 percent of emergency rooms did not meet the minimal recommendations of six air changes per hour, negative air pressure, and air exhausted to the outside of the building.[7] If that's the situation in medical facilities, what's happening in nursing homes, homeless shelters, and prisons?

Some people have also accused immigrants of spreading HIV/AIDS. In the early 1980s, many news reports questioned whether the HIV virus had come to the United States from Africa via Haiti. Being Haitian was even considered a risk factor in itself, a label that led to the stigmatization of Haitian immigrants.

Dr. Jean William Pape, who treated Haiti's first AIDS cases, found that in fact, the disease was likely brought to Haiti by U.S. tourists.[8]

In 1987, Philippine Health Department statistics found that the heaviest concentration of AIDS cases in that country was among prostitutes working near two U.S. military bases, Clark Air Base and Subic Bay Naval Base—suggesting that HIV had been introduced there by U.S. soldiers.[9] The issue spurred local opposition to the bases, which were closed in 1992.

Still, U.S. immigration policy officially bans foreign nationals who are infected with HIV from entering the United States or gaining status as legal immigrants—even though "there is no public health rationale for restricting liberty of movement or choice of residence on the grounds of HIV status," according to the United Nations International Guidelines on HIV/AIDS and Human Rights.[10]

Is immigration bad for the environment?

The environment is global—it doesn't stop at national boundaries. Immigration has no impact on any of the major environmental threats facing us, such as global climate change, deforestation, radioactive and chemical waste, and air and water pollution.

It's true that the clandestine crossing of large numbers of migrants across remote border areas has hurt the local environment in those areas, especially in the Arizona desert. But trash left by border walkers (empty water bottles, discarded clothing, and such) is not a major ecological problem; it could easily be cleaned up by volunteer crews over a couple of days. Tracks cut through the desert and mountains by smugglers' vehicles cause longer-term damage, but if we could allow people a way to come here legally, through airports and established border posts, we would avoid such problems.

Enforcement makes the problem worse: Border Patrol vehicles tear up the desert, night lighting disturbs wildlife habitats, and every new wall or fence blocks animal migration while pushing people farther into the most remote areas with the most fragile ecosystems. The United States-Mexico border region is home to many endangered species—including jaguars, wolves, bears, parrots, and low-flying owls—that need to move around as an essential element of their survival.[11]

Some environmentalists support the construction of special barriers that keep vehicles out while allowing wildlife (and people) to cross. Scientists fear that a new 700-mile border fence designed to block migrants from crossing, included in legeslation signed by President George W. Bush in October 2006, will spell environmental disaster.[12]

Do immigrants care about the environment?

Environmental degradation disproportionately affects low-income African American, Native American, and Latino communities. Farm laborers and their families are exposed to pesticides in the fields, nearby homes, and schools. Disenfranchised urban communities and isolated rural ones are poisoned by toxic dumps. Immigrant factory workers go unprotected while handling dangerous chemicals.

These low-income communities are also leading the fight to clean up their environment. In 1990, grassroots organizations representing immigrant and non-immigrant people of color in the southwestern United States formed the Southwest Network for Environmental and Economic Justice to join together in fighting toxins in their communities.[13] In 1994, the mostly Latino residents of Kettleman City, California, won a six-year battle against the Chemical Waste Management (ChemWaste) corporation's plans to put a hazardous waste incinerator in their town. The campaign included a lawsuit, filed in 1991 by a coalition of farmworkers and other community members, challenging the fact that meetings and notifications in the permit process for the incinerator were only in English.[14]

Are immigrants to blame for population growth?

Some people blame immigrants for U.S. population growth, and try to stir up alarm about the issue.

Most of this country's recent population growth has been among people who are not of white European descent—particularly Latin Americans, who generally have some combination of indigenous, European, and African heritage. So when people express fear that the U.S. population is spiraling out of control, they often mean they feel uncomfortable about increasing numbers of people in their area who they perceive as different from themselves.

Such fears have been exploited by white supremacists like David Duke, who proclaimed on his website: "I will fight to limit overpopulation and protect our environment by stopping illegal immigration and almost all legal immigration into America."[15]

Is overpopulation a serious environmental threat?

Population growth in itself is not a major cause of environmental problems. "In many countries, population growth rates have declined yet environmental conditions continue to deteriorate," the Committee on Women, Population and the Environment (CWPE) noted in 1992.[16]

For one thing, wealthy people have a disproportionate impact on the environment compared to poor people. The United States, with less than 5 percent of the global population, uses about a quarter of the world's fossil fuel resources. Within every country, wealthy people consume considerably more resources than poor people, and generate more pollution.[17]

The environmental impact even of wasteful U.S. households pales compared to that of industry and military operations. The U.S. military is the world's largest single polluter, generating an estimated 750,000 tons of toxic waste annually, more than the five largest chemical companies in the United States combined.[18]

How can we slow population growth?

Reducing immigration doesn't affect global population growth, because like the environment, population is not defined by national borders.

Population growth in particular countries goes up or down based on a number of factors. Mexico's population grew dramatically during the twentieth century, for example, from fifteen million in 1910 to 105.3 million by the middle of 2004. This happened because better health care and sanitation meant that older people lived longer and more children lived to become adults; the annual death rate fell by two-thirds from 1910 to 1970. Since then, access to family planning and improved opportunities for women have brought the birth rate down. In 1976 the average Mexican woman was having about 5.7 children in her lifetime; by 2005 the birth rate had fallen to 2.1 children for the average woman, just a little more than enough to keep the population constant.[19]

"Demographic data from around the globe affirm that improvements in women's social, economic and health status and in general living standards are often keys to declines in population growth rates," the Committee on Women, Population and the Environment pointed out in 1992.[20]

In order to stem population growth, the United States should "address the root causes of migration in our foreign policy and work with our neighbors to help improve educational and economic opportunities for people," wrote Brian Dixon, government affairs director of the nonprofit group Population Connection, in November 2006.[21]

What about overcrowding in our communities?

The overcrowding of certain urban or suburban areas is impacted as much by internal migration and economic changes as by immigration from abroad. Corporations turn once industrial cities into ghost towns by moving their factories overseas to profit from cheaper labor. Seniors resettle in retirement communities. Rural people move to the cities; urban residents move to the suburbs. Real estate developers transform rural landscapes into urban sprawl. Schools, public transportation, hospitals, and other services are often slow to accommodate such rapid changes. Community members aren't consulted, and their needs are left unmet.

Such problems can be confronted by communities joining together and organizing to demand adequate services. Most immigrants come here for a better future—they don't want to live with overcrowded schools, traffic jams, or garbage dumps any more than U.S.-born citizens do.

In 1992, parents in an adult education class launched a campaign to reform the public schools in their south Bronx neighborhood. The campaign gave birth to Mothers on the Move, which has brought together the community's diverse residents—including Puerto Ricans, African Americans, and recent immigrants—to win battles for better schools, affordable housing, clean air, and safe streets.[22]

Do immigrants learn English?

In 1751 Benjamin Franklin warned that German immigration would destroy the English language in Pennsylvania. "[I]n a few years," he wrote, Pennsylvania would "become a German colony; instead of their learning our language, we must learn theirs, or live as in a foreign country."[23]

There's no evidence that immigrants now are slower to learn English than the immigrants that came before them. According to the 2000 U.S. Census, about 65 percent of the foreign-born over the age of five speak English "very well" or "well"; 23 percent speak English "not well," and 12 percent speak it "not at all."

To many people it may *seem* that there are more and more foreigners who don't speak English, since the number of the foreign born who speak a language other than English has increased by 65 percent since 1990—just a little more than the rate at which the immigrant population has increased since 1990.[24]

In fact, immigrants are eager to learn English. Nonprofit organizations that provide free or low-cost English classes are generally swamped with students. According to a June 2006 study, a large group that teaches English as a second language (ESL) in Phoenix, Arizona, reported an eighteen-month waiting period for some evening classes. In Boston, at least 16,725 adults were on waiting lists for ESL classes, and waiting times for some programs were close to three years; New York City programs had waiting periods of up to several years.[25]

Are the new immigrants too "different" to assimilate?

While it's obvious that immigrants in the nineteenth and early twentieth centuries adapted to U.S. culture, some people argue that these immigrants could assimilate easily because most were Europeans. The new immigrants are overwhelmingly from Latin America and Asia, places with cultures that are supposedly more "alien" than European cultures in the earlier period.

The evidence doesn't support this. James Smith of the California-based Rand Corporation, a conservative think tank that often produces analyses for the U.S. government, studied three generations of Mexicans in the United States and found that their rate of educational progress—a good measure of cultural assimilation—was the same or greater than that of Europeans who immigrated in the late nineteenth and early twentieth century.[26]

Actually, people from Latin America and Asia now are probably less "alien" than Eastern or Southern Europeans were a hundred years ago, due to increased global communication and heavy promotion by U.S. entertainment companies of their products. For example, most people in Asia and Latin America were already regularly viewing U.S. television programs by the late 1970s and early 1980s.[27]

At the same time, the United States is more and more influenced by non-European cultures: we eat sushi, learn karate or tai chi, consider tacos to be "American" food, and listen to singers of Latin American origin on the radio.

A 1997 report on immigration by the National Academy of Sciences noted that European immigrants in the past were "once so distinct as to be referred to as 'races.' " But now their "children, grandchildren and great-grandchildren...have intermarried to such an extent as to virtually erase differences in education, income, occupation, and residence."[28]

What factors slow assimilation?

Throughout U.S. history immigrants—especially those from outside Europe—have faced exclusion, discrimination, and outright violence. Instead of integrating Chinese immigrants into U.S. society, immigration opponents denied them the right to become naturalized citizens in the 1870 Naturalization Act, barred them from bringing their families to the United States, organized violent attacks on them, and segregated them into "Chinatowns." Other Asian immigrants were also barred from becoming citizens, and California banned Japanese immigrants from owning land in 1913. During the Second World War, the federal government confined 120,000 Japanese Americans, most of them native-born U.S. citizens, in "internment camps."[29]

This country's black-and-white "race" prism also affects assimilation. Immigrants who seem to be of European or African descent are perceived to be "American" as soon as they no longer have a "foreign" accent, while people who "look" Asian or Latino are seen as foreign, even if their families have been here for generations. In the memoir *Black Cuban, Black American*, Evelio Grillo recounts his youth growing up in the 1920s and 1930s in Tampa, Florida, and attending segregated black schools, where he learned African-American history and was transformed from a Cuban immigrant into a "black American."[30]

Who are the "real Americans"?

If there is such a thing as "real Americans," those who have the most right to that claim are the descendants of the millions of people who were living in North America when the Europeans first arrived. The Europeans who settled here adopted many things from the Native Americans, including: canoes; crops like corn, squash, and tobacco; and the use of buckskins for clothing. Slaves brought here by force from Africa also shaped U.S. culture with stories, words, and music that reflect West African traditions as well as their struggles to survive and escape slavery in the "New World."

The English were latecomers to what is now the United States. The first European settlers came from Spain—this country's oldest continuous settlement is Saint Augustine, which the United States acquired when it purchased Florida from Spain in 1819. Texas and California and the southwestern states were part of Mexico, making up about 51 percent of Mexican territory. The United States annexed Texas in 1845 and took control of the rest as its spoils from the U.S.-Mexican War of 1846–1848. Some 200,000 Native Americans inhabited these territories at the time; so did 100,000 Mexican nationals, most of them Spanish-speaking and many of them *mestizos*, people of mixed Spanish and indigenous ancestry.[31]

Like these first Mexican Americans, many Latin Americans who immigrate here trace at least part of their ancestry to the hemisphere's indigenous peoples, who likely came to this continent from Asia thousands or maybe tens of thousands of years before any Europeans arrived in the Western Hemisphere.

Many U.S. place-names reflect the diversity of origins that make up "real America." Throughout the country, hundreds of place-names come from indigenous languages, including the names of at least twenty-one of our fifty states. Several other states get their names from Spanish. Most of California's best-known cities have Spanish names, including San Francisco, Los Angeles, and Sacramento.

8

Are Immigrants a Threat?

Do immigrants commit more crimes than non-immigrants?

"Few stereotypes of immigrants are as enduring, or have been proven so categorically false over literally decades of research, as the notion that immigrants are disproportionately likely to engage in criminal activity," stated a 1997 paper jointly sponsored by two Washington-based nonpartisan research organizations, the Carnegie Endowment for International Peace and the Urban Institute. In fact, the results of these decades of research "are surprisingly unambiguous: immigrants are disproportionately unlikely to be criminal."[1]

A 1998 study analyzed Federal Bureau of Investigation (FBI) Uniform Crime Reports and Census Bureau data from several dozen U.S. metropolitan areas and confirmed that recent immigrants had no significant effect either on crime rates or the change in rates over time. The authors also analyzed data from the National Longitudinal Survey of Youth and found that young people born abroad were significantly less likely than native-born youths to be criminally active.[2]

Why does the myth of immigrant crime persist? One factor may be the impact of media coverage on public perceptions of crime and criminals. A study published in 2002 in the *Journal of Research in Crime and Delinquency* reviewed television newscasts over a three-week period in Orlando, Florida, and found that 28 percent of all "Hispanics" (people of Latin-American origin) appearing on the news did so in the role of criminal suspect—more than twice the rate for African Americans and 5.6 times the rate for whites. Both African Americans and "Hispanics" were presented as criminal suspects four times as often as they were presented as crime victims.[3]

While many "Hispanics" are not immigrants, and many immigrants are not from Latin America, there is a general tendency for people to equate the two, so it's likely that any public perception about "Hispanics" will translate into a perception of immigrants.

Crime data are generally based on arrest or conviction statistics—they don't tell us who *commits* crimes, just who *gets caught*. White youths—including those who are middle class and wealthy—probably commit as much crime as African-American and Latino youths (maybe more, since they have less fear of consequences). Yet police don't routinely follow, stop, question, and search white youths the way they do African-American and Latino youths—and in some areas, Native-American and Asian youths (especially Cambodians, Vietnamese, and Samoans).

"And Justice for Some," a comprehensive national report by the National Council on Crime and Delinquency, found that youths of color are treated more severely than white youths at every stage of the justice system—from arrest to incarceration—even when charged with the same offenses.[4] For youths charged with drug offenses, the incarceration rate for Latino youths was thirteen times the rate for white youths.[5]

Is it unfair to treat immigrants who commit crimes differently than citizens?

Immigrant non-citizens who are arrested for crimes pose no more of a threat to society than do U.S. citizens accused of the same crimes. Yet many non-citizens, even if they are longtime permanent legal residents, face a much harsher consequence for those crimes—after completing their sentences, they are held in immigration jails for weeks, months, or even years, and are then usually deported.

Often the distinction between a citizen and a non-citizen seems arbitrary. Take Sacha Sealey, who enlisted in the U.S. Army at age 17 in 1983, and took part in the U.S. invasion of Grenada in October of that year. After two years of service, Sealey suffered from post-traumatic stress disorder, and like many combat veterans, he struggled with addiction. But Sealey was born in Canada, and although he had been living legally in the United States since he was a toddler, he never got around to seeking citizenship. "I figured my card said 'permanent residence,' that's permanent not temporary. I didn't think there was that much of a difference," Sealey later told a reporter for the Long Island paper *Newsday*. Sealey pleaded guilty to a few minor drug arrests, without realizing they would result in deportation. He had spent 10 months in a rehab center and was fighting to get his life back together when he went to the immigration office to renew his green card on June 30, 2003. There Sealey was handcuffed and thrown into immigration detention. For eight months he endured harsh conditions in New Jersey county jails. While he was detained, his sister died, leaving his widowed mother alone in Queens, New York. In March 2004, Sealey was deported to Montreal, barred from ever returning legally to the United States.[6]

For immigrants who have established their lives in the United States, deportation is exile—a cruel punishment that is not imposed on U.S. citizens. Most of those who are deported for crimes have committed minor, victimless offenses; they don't deserve such a harsh penalty. Many immigrants, like Sacha Sealey, came here as children. They are indistinguishable in every way from most U.S.-born citizens. If they get involved in drugs or commit crimes, it's something they learned here, in the United States—not in their "native" country. Some don't even remember the country where they were born, don't speak the language, have no family or friends there, and once deported, are unable to adjust.

Does deportation make us safer?

Deporting someone for a violent crime may actually make us less safe. Deportees are no longer in the system; no one is monitoring them to make sure they don't violate their parole conditions. They may remain in their country of birth, or they may manage to slip back into the United States, but either way, they're off the radar screen. Public safety is also jeopardized when witnesses to crime—or victims of it—are deported.

Some victims of violent crime may still feel safer knowing that the perpetrator has been deported and is far away in another country. But the vast majority of people who commit violent crimes are U.S. citizens, and no such comfort is available to their victims. All victims of violent crime deserve justice, and measures to protect their safety, regardless of whether their victimizer was a U.S. citizen or an immigrant.

Deporting alleged terrorists doesn't make much sense either. If we actually suspect someone of terrorism, shouldn't that person face trial in a criminal court, instead of being deported for minor immigration violations? Would you feel safer, knowing that a suspected terrorist had been sent to another country, rather than being prosecuted?

Is there a link between immigration and terrorism?

There is no connection between immigration and terrorism. Yet since September 11, 2001, when coordinated terror attacks left some 3,000 people dead in the northeastern United States, the image of terrorists as Muslim foreigners has held a persistent grip on this country's national consciousness.

The nineteen suspected perpetrators of the 9/11 attacks all came here from other countries and were Muslims. (There were also more than 500 foreign-born people, and at least fifty-nine Muslims, among the victims.)[7] But the second-most deadly terrorism attack of all time on U.S. soil was carried out by a white, U.S.-born citizen and Gulf War veteran, Timothy McVeigh. That bombing killed 168 people, including nineteen children, at the federal building in Oklahoma City on April 19, 1995.

No one suggests that white Gulf War veterans should be singled out for special scrutiny or arrested as suspicious when they approach federal buildings. So why should foreigners—especially those who are Muslims, or of Arab or South Asian descent—be treated as terrorists?

Is the government going after foreign terrorists?

On its website lifeandliberty.gov, which as of October 2006 appeared not to have been updated in at least seven months, the U.S. Justice Department claimed to have prosecuted 401 people in "terrorism-related investigations" since September 11, winning convictions or guilty pleas in more than 212 cases. In June 2005, the *Washington Post* examined those 212 convictions and found that only thirty-nine cases involved charges related to terrorism. Of those thirty-nine cases, most involved "broad-based charges of association with, or support of, a terrorist group, without any connection to actual terrorist actions," according to Georgetown University law professor David Cole.[8]

After reviewing prosecutions in "terror-related" cases, New York University's Center on Law and Security concluded that: "the legal war on terror has yielded few visible results. There have been...almost no convictions on charges reflecting dangerous crimes."[9]

The Justice Department also claimed, on its website, to have deported more than 515 foreign nationals linked to the investigation of the September 11 attacks. In fact, most of the deportations were carried out under a policy that barred deportation unless a person was first cleared by the FBI of any connection to terrorism.[10] In a February 2003 letter, FBI agent Coleen Rowley complained to her boss, FBI director Robert Mueller, that following the September 11 attacks the agency's headquarters "encouraged more and more detentions" of out-of-status immigrants "for what seemed to be essentially PR purposes," in order to create the appearance of "progress in fighting terrorism."[11]

Through a "special registration" program, started in September 2002, the immigration service fingerprinted, photographed, and questioned 80,000 male immigrants from twenty-four predominantly Muslim countries and North Korea. Another 8,000 people—mainly Arab and Muslim men—were interviewed by the FBI. At least 5,000 immigrants were detained—nearly all of them on minor immigration violations—in alleged connection to anti-terrorism investigations. None of the people swept up in these programs was ever convicted of a terrorist crime. "In what has surely been the most aggressive national campaign of ethnic profiling since World War II," notes Professor Cole, "the government's record is 0 for 93,000."

Meanwhile, terrorism has apparently grown internationally. In June 2004, the U.S. State Department admitted that the number of injuries resulting from international terrorist incidents had risen from 2,013 in 2002 to 3,646 in 2003. In 2005, the State Department eliminated numbers from its annual terrorism report, claiming they were "too difficult to track accurately," according to Cole; in fact, Cole reports, "government analysts had found that terrorist incidents worldwide had jumped threefold from 2003 levels, with 651 attacks in 2004 resulting in 1,907 deaths."[12]

How did the September 11 hijackers get here?

All nineteen of the suspected 9/11 hijackers came to the United States legally on valid visas, and once here, only two violated the terms of their visas. Fifteen were from Saudi Arabia, and two were from the United Arab Emirates; both countries are wealthy oil nations with close ties to the U.S. government. (The other two suspects were Egyptian and Lebanese, but got their visas at the U.S. embassy in Berlin.) As a 2003 report from the Migration Policy Institute points out, even under the strictest immigration controls, most of the hijackers would still be allowed into the United States today. They had been "carefully chosen to avoid detection: all but two were educated young men from middle-class families with no criminal records and no known connection to terrorism."[13]

In fact, the suspected hijackers did not face much scrutiny. U.S. diplomatic posts in Saudi Arabia had a policy of calling in fewer than 2 percent of visa applicants for interviews, and granting visas to nearly everyone who applied (only 3 percent of applicants were turned down in fiscal years 2000 and 2001, according to State Department figures). A similar policy was in place for the United Arab Emirates.[14]

When the General Accounting Office (GAO), the nonpartisan investigative arm of Congress, reviewed the visa applications submitted by fifteen of the suspected hijackers in Saudi Arabia and the United Arab Emirates, it found that not one of the suspects had filled in the documents properly, and only two had been interviewed. (The applications for the four other suspects were destroyed before investigators could review them.)[15]

Who decides who's a terrorist?

The people deported in the post-9/11 "anti-terrorism" sweeps have been immigrants or students who the government has falsely tried to paint as terrorists. But one person fighting deportation in 2006 was Cuban-born Luis Posada Carriles, a longtime asset of the U.S. Central Intelligence Agency (CIA) who is believed to have orchestrated the 1976 bombing of a Cuban passenger jet that killed seventy-three people—a crime that by any standard should be considered terrorism. "If Luis Posada Carriles does not meet the definition of a terrorist, it is hard to think of who would," observed Peter Kornbluh, director of the Cuba Documentation Project at the independent National Security Archive (NSA).

It shouldn't be hard to charge Posada, or to send him to face trial in one of the countries where his crimes took place. But as of October 2006, the U.S. government was ignoring requests from Venezuela for his extradition, and declining to officially designate him as a terrorist, which would technically allow them to hold him under the 2001 USA PATRIOT Act. Posada's Texas lawyer pointed out the U.S. government's dilemma: "How can you call someone a terrorist who allegedly committed acts on your behalf?"[16]

In the 1980s, the United States made special visa arrangements to train terrorists to fight the Soviet Union's occupation of Afghanistan, according to Michael Springman, who headed the U.S. visa bureau in the Saudi Arabian city of Jeddah from 1987 to 1989. Springman said he was "repeatedly ordered by high-level State Department officials to issue visas to unqualified applicants," many of whom were not Saudi citizens and couldn't explain why they wanted to visit the United States.[17] In one case, Springman said, a refugee from Sudan who was unemployed in Saudi Arabia got a visa "for National Security purposes, after it was taken out of my hands by the chief of the consular section."[18] Springman said he eventually learned that the visas were being facilitated as part of a CIA program "to bring recruits, rounded up by [Saudi terrorist leader] Osama Bin Laden, to the United States for terrorist training by the CIA. They would then be returned to Afghanistan to fight against the then-Soviets."[19]

"One country's terrorist can often be another country's freedom fighter," noted Judge John Noonan in a December 2003 decision for the Ninth Circuit Court of Appeals, pointing out that the U.S. government had backed the right-wing *contra* fighters in Nicaragua, who also engaged in acts of terrorism. Noonan ordered immigration officials to release Harpal Singh Cheema, a Sikh activist from India who had been held on secret evidence since November 1997. "It is by no means self-evident that a person engaged in extra-territorial or resistance activities—even militant activities—is necessarily a threat to the security of the United States," wrote Noonan.[20]

But the U.S. government considered Singh a terrorist, not a freedom fighter, and kept him jailed in California for more than eight years, much of that time in solitary confinement. Singh finally gave up his fight against deportation and agreed to return to India, where he had been tortured in the past. He was deported in April 2006, and as of August 2006 remained jailed in India's Punjab region.[21]

The Mirmehdi brothers, four Iranians living in southern California, were detained for nearly four years; the immigration agency claimed they were members of a terrorist group, the Mujahedin-e Khalq (MEK). Two of the brothers had attended a June 1997 demonstration in Denver organized by the National Council of Resistance of Iran (NCR), a coalition linked to the MEK. It wasn't until four months later, in October, that the State Department added the MEK to its list of terrorist organizations.[22]

The NCR continued to enjoy the support of at least 200 members of the U.S. Congress—even after the State Department added the coalition to the terrorist list in 1999, claiming it was another name for the MEK. When the NCR held a rally in front of the United Nations in New York in September 2000, Missouri's two Republican senators sent a written statement of solidarity that was read aloud to the crowd, *Newsweek* reported in 2002. One of the two senators was John Ashcroft, who became attorney general in 2002 and fought to block the Mirmehdi brothers' release on bond. (A Justice Department spokesperson later claimed Ashcroft's statement of solidarity did not "intend to endorse any organization.")[23]

The Mirmehdi brothers were finally released in March 2005—a month after Ashcroft left office, and as their case began to draw wider media attention. "This shouldn't happen in the United States," Mostafa Mirmehdi said of his family's ordeal. "If it took place in Iran, I would expect it, but I came here for freedom."[24]

Does the crackdown on immigrants make us safer?

In 2002, six immigration experts—including former Immigration and Naturalization Service (INS) commissioner Doris Meissner—conducted an eighteen-month review of post-September 11 immigration measures for the Migration Policy Institute. Their June 2003 report found that the post-9/11 crackdown on immigrants has actually put this country at greater risk by diverting resources away from in-depth, responsible intelligence work, and by alienating and intimidating communities that could help with terrorism investigations.

Specifically, the report criticizes the Justice Department's "efforts to enlist state and local law enforcement agencies into enforcing federal immigration law" as counterproductive to community safety and the fight against terrorism. "Such action undercuts the trust that local law enforcement agencies have built with immigrant communities, making immigrants less likely to report crimes, come forward as witnesses, or provide intelligence information, out of fear that they or their families risk detention or deportation."

The report also condemns the government's unchecked use of immigration detention in anti-terrorism cases. "Arresting a large number of noncitizens on grounds not related to domestic security only gives the nation a false sense of security," the report notes.[25]

How does the crackdown on immigrants affect the rest of us?

The Migration Policy Institute's June 2003 report argues that the government violated the First Amendment's protection of the public's right to be informed about government actions by deliberately hiding the identity, number, and whereabouts of immigrant detainees following the 9/11 attacks. "This right is at the heart of our democracy, and is crucial to maintaining government accountability to the public," says the report.

By targeting specific ethnic groups with its post-9/11 immigrant operations, the government also violated the Fifth Amendment's guarantee of equal protection. After reviewing the cases of 406 post-9/11 immigrant detainees and interviewing community leaders, lawyers, and advocates, the Migration Policy

Institute concluded that many detainees were picked up "because of profiling by ordinary citizens, who called government agencies about neighbors, coworkers and strangers based on their ethnicity or appearance." The report notes that "law enforcement agencies selectively followed up on such tips for persons of Arab or Muslim extraction."[26]

People who are not targeted by the post-9/11 sweeps may feel it doesn't affect them. But if such profiling is left unchallenged, where will it end? As the much-quoted statement of German pastor Martin Niemöller, describing the Nazi government's pattern of targeted arrests, warns us:

> First they came for the Communists, but I was not a Communist, so I did not speak out. Then they came for the Socialists and the Trade Unionists, but I was neither, so I did not speak out. Then they came for the Jews, but I was not a Jew, so I did not speak out. And when they came for me, there was no one left to speak out for me.[27]

Did all this start with September 11?

"The government's post-September 11 actions follow a repeating pattern in [U.S.] history of rounding up immigrant groups during national security crises," warned the Migration Policy Institute's 2003 report. "Like the internment of Japanese Americans during World War II, the deportation of Eastern European immigrants during the Red Scare of 1919–20, and the harassment and internment of German Americans during World War I, these actions will come to be seen as a stain on America's heritage as a nation of immigrants and a land where individual rights are valued and protected."[28]

In 1952, anti-communists in Congress pushed through the Immigration and Nationality Act (INA), also known as the McCarran-Walter act. The INA became the new body of immigration law, incorporating or replacing all previous laws with new provisions making it easier to detain immigrants, deny them release on bail, and deport them for alleged "subversion." The act allowed immigrants to be excluded or deported based on purely ideological grounds, and barred "aliens afflicted with psychopathic personality, epilepsy, or mental defect"—a category expressly created by Congress to exclude what it called "homosexuals and sex perverts." Most of the ideological provisions—along with the ban on homosexuals—were formally repealed by Congress in 1990, although many were reincorporated in the USA PATRIOT Act of 2001.[29]

In January 1987, under the administration of Ronald Reagan, the federal government arrested a group of eight activists for Palestinian rights in Los Angeles and tried to deport them under the INA's anti-communism provisions, using secret evidence. The "Los Angeles Eight" fought back through the courts. Twenty years later, at the end of 2006, two of them—both legal residents at the time of their arrest—were still fighting the government's efforts to deport them.[30] Secret evidence is not allowed in criminal cases, but under the 1952 law the government is permitted to use it to block non-citizens from gaining political asylum, permanent residence, naturalization, or release on bond.

In 1997, under the administration of Bill Clinton, Attorney General Janet Reno used provisions of the INA to justify the detention of at least twenty immigrants—nearly all of them Arabs—on secret evidence. (Secret evidence was also used in at least two immigration cases involving members of the Irish Republican Army, but Reno suspended these cases in September 1997 after the State Department suggested that pursuing them could disrupt the peace process in Northern Ireland.)[31]

Several of the Clinton-era secret evidence cases—including that of Sikh activist Harpal Singh Cheema—lingered into the post-9/11 scenario. Palestinian scholar Mazen Al-Najjar was detained on secret evidence for three and a half years by the Clinton administration; he was released in December 2000 after a judge ruled the evidence against him was insufficient and his detention was unconstitutional. He was rearrested by the Bush administration in November 2001, and held in solitary confinement for nine months until he was deported in August 2002.[32]

The Bush administration's post-9/11 secret detentions surpassed the Clinton-era ones in numbers: at least 1,200 people were swept up. As Georgetown University law professor David Cole observed, "Never in our history has the government engaged in such a blanket practice of secret incarceration."[33]

Are immigrant workers a national security risk?

Many people have prejudiced ideas about Muslim, Arab, and south Asian immigrants, which politicians and government officials seem to encourage and exploit to build support for "anti-terrorism" efforts. But most people don't associate Mexican laborers or Haitian refugees with terrorism.

That hasn't stopped officials from trying to justify a broader crackdown on immigrant workers in the name of the "war on terror." In press releases describing the arrest of workers at "critical infrastructure" sites like airports and military bases, the U.S. Immigration and Customs Enforcement (ICE) agency acknowledges that the workers aren't terrorists, but claims they are a security risk because their undocumented status and use of false documents makes them vulnerable to blackmail by terrorists. (Other potential blackmail risks, such as workers who are cheating on their spouses, don't seem to spark that concern—although the same reasoning was used until recently to argue against allowing gay people to work in sensitive jobs.)

In April 2003, then-Attorney General John Ashcroft tried to extend the national security argument to refugees fleeing Haiti by issuing a legal opinion defending the continued detention without bond of 18-year-old Haitian asylum-seeker David Joseph. Ashcroft claimed that releasing Haitians like Joseph could trigger a wave of immigration by sea, threatening national security by overtaxing the Coast Guard, Border Patrol, and other agencies focused on preventing terror attacks. Ashcroft also claimed the government had noticed an increase in Pakistanis and Palestinians "using Haiti as a staging point for attempted migration to the United States." That claim baffled the State Department's Consular Service. "We all are scratching our heads," said spokesperson Stuart Patt. "We are asking each other, 'Where did they get that?' "[34]

9

Enforcement: Is It a Solution?

If we enforce our laws, will the problem go away?

It's not at all clear that immigration—even unauthorized immigration—is a problem. But enforcement is certainly not a solution. Drug enforcement has not helped to curb addiction (which unlike immigration, has a negative impact on society).[1] Enforcement tactics waste taxpayer money, violate people's human rights, and generate greater profits for those involved in the trafficking underworld. Drug enforcement makes drug smugglers rich, and immigration enforcement makes people smugglers rich. When one trafficker is jailed, others step in to take the customers and the profits. And there are always corrupt government agents willing to help the trade prosper.

Enforcement creates more problems than it solves. To address complex issues like immigration we have to look at the root causes, such as poverty, war, and human rights abuses abroad.

What if we deport all the "illegal" immigrants?

The estimated twelve million out-of-status immigrants living in the United States are an integral part of our country. They are our family members, friends, partners, co-workers, classmates, and neighbors. Efforts to deport them all would rip apart the fabric of our society.

Mass deportations would also be expensive. In 1986, when Congress decided to extend amnesty, or limited legalization, to undocumented immigrants, one of the main reasons Congress members gave was the difficulty of deporting the unauthorized population, then less than half as large as in 2006. Representative Peter Rodino, a New Jersey Democrat, said he supported amnesty because, "In my judgment, we cannot deport these people. We would not, I am sure, provide the money to conduct the raids. It would mean billions of dollars in order to try to deport them...."[2]

Opinion polls show the U.S. public deeply split on the question of immigration, so we can guess that at least half the population probably wouldn't support efforts to deport twelve million immigrants, and a good number might actively oppose such a drastic move.[3] That resistance would certainly grow at the sight of federal agents trampling roughshod over families and communities. It's one thing to have a discussion about the pros and cons of immigration, but political views aside, most people don't want to see their friends and neighbors led off in shackles just because of their immigration status.

On September 1, 2006, federal agents began rounding up out-of-status immigrants in Stillmore, Georgia. The community of 1,000 people lost some 120 residents—more than 10 percent of its population—in the raids, and hundreds more fled, turning Stillmore into a ghost town. David Robinson, who operates a trailer park in town, watched helplessly as the agents handcuffed residents and hauled them away. To protest, he bought a U.S. flag and posted it upside down in front of the trailer park. "These people might not have American rights, but they've damn sure got human rights," Robinson said. "There ain't no reason to treat them like animals."[4]

Are we doing enough to secure the border?

Like other forms of enforcement, border crackdowns are largely ineffective, and cause more problems than they solve. In fact, the U.S. government has been stepping up its efforts to stop unauthorized entry at the border with Mexico since the early 1990s—at the same time it was negotiating the NAFTA trade pact with Mexico. In 1990, the U.S. Border Patrol started construction of a ten-foot-high welded steel fence along fourteen miles of the southwest border near San Diego, California, one of the main entry points for immigrants who enter the United States without permission.[5]

By the end of 1994, under the administration of President Bill Clinton, the Border Patrol had started three major enforcement operations at the Mexican border, using fences, barriers, hi-tech surveillance methods, and an expanded force of agents: Operation Blockade (later renamed Hold the Line) in El Paso, Texas; Operation Gatekeeper in San Diego; and Operation Safeguard around Nogales, Arizona. In 1997, the Border Patrol initiated Operation Rio Grande, in Brownsville, Texas. During this period, from 1993 to 1998, the number of Border Patrol agents in the Southwest more than doubled from 3,389 to 7,357, and the annual cost to taxpayers rose from about $400 million in 1993 to $800 million in 1997.[6]

By 2006 the number of border agents had risen to about 12,000, from 2,500 in the early 1980s; the Border Patrol's annual budget had jumped to $1.6 billion, eight times the $200 million budget two decades before.[7] And the Border Patrol is only part of the agency that handles border enforcement; President George W. Bush's proposed budget for the Customs and Border Protection agency in fiscal year 2007 was $7.8 billion, a 9.83 percent increase over the year before.[8]

What has border enforcement done so far?

The U.S. government uses the number of apprehensions of unauthorized border crossers to gauge the flow of undocumented immigrants. By this measure, the various enforcement operations of the 1990s did almost nothing to slow unauthorized entry: the total arrests on the southwest border were 1.3 million in 1995 and 1.2 million in 2005.[9]

But the new operations had a worse record than these figures indicate. The number of unauthorized immigrants in the United States rose by some five million from 1990 to 2000, at a significantly faster rate than in previous decades, and continued to rise almost as quickly afterwards. In January 2001, Alex Aleinikoff, a former general counsel for the now-defunct Immigration and Naturalization Service, warned that programs like Operation Gatekeeper weren't working. "Operation Gatekeeper has become our Vietnam," he said. Immigration service officials were "mistakenly thinking that if we added just a little more [to the buildup], then a little more, that we would get results."[10]

The enforcement operations did cut illegal border crossings near urban areas like San Diego and El Paso, but the main effect was just "squeezing the balloon"—forcing immigrants to change their routes and methods. One result was that more migrants started hiring professional smugglers, at higher rates. From 1994 to 2005 the average price for being smuggled through the San Diego area jumped from $300 to $2,500; the cost of being smuggled through the Arizona desert rose to as much as $1,800.[11]

Another result is that people started trying to avoid the enforcement zones by crossing through more remote and often dangerous terrain. According to the Tijuana-based Colegio de la Frontera Norte, a research organization focusing on border issues, about 3,700 people died between 1994 and 2006 while attempting to cross the border, mostly along these new, riskier routes.[12] In the year ending September 30, 2005, the U.S. government logged a record-breaking 473 migrant deaths at the border.[13] Wayne Cornelius, a professor of Political Science at the University of California, San Diego, notes that the death toll at the border from 1994 to 2004 was more than ten times as high as the number of people killed trying to cross the Berlin Wall in its twenty-eight-year history.[14]

U.S. officials expected these results from increased enforcement. Alan Bersin, the Clinton administration official in charge of southwest border policy from 1995 to 1998, described the policy as "forc[ing] migrants into much more inhospitable and rugged places," adding that "the difficulty of passage is evidenced in the increased number of accidents and fatalities involving illegal entrants."[15]

Migrants are more likely to die while crossing remote sectors of the border, but they are also less likely to be caught—so the stepped-up enforcement actually decreases the odds that migrants are apprehended while attempting to enter the United States.[16]

Increased border enforcement has also had the paradoxical effect of keeping more out-of-status immigrants from leaving the United States. Because of the greater danger and expense of entering, the undocumented are now less likely than in the past to work here a few months and then return home for a period—instead, they stay here longer or settle down. According to Princeton sociology professor Douglas S. Massey, in the 1980s about half of all undocumented Mexicans returned home within twelve months of entry, but by 2000 the rate of return migration stood at just 25 percent.[17] "If that is what is going on," UC, San Diego professor Cornelius wrote in 2004, "it means that the U.S. border-centered immigration control strategy has been effective in bottling up illegal migrants within the United States, not necessarily in deterring them from coming in the first place."[18]

Can't we seal off the border?

Politicians regularly call for controlling the border by building more fencing or deploying military troops. But such measures are expensive, and have a high human and environmental cost: border walls endanger fragile ecosystems, and militarization poses a serious threat to the safety of migrants and residents of border communities.

The U.S. Army Corps of Engineers estimates that a double-layer fence along the 2,000-mile border with Mexico would cost $1.2–1.3 million a mile for construction, a total of about $2.4 billion. But this estimate doesn't cover the cost of labor (to be supplied by the Department of Defense), or of buying the land (mostly in Texas, since the federal government owns much of the border land further west). According to the Department of Homeland Security, the current fourteen-mile San Diego fence cost $127 million, or $9 million a mile; at that rate, a fence for the whole border would cost $18 billion (although the department claims there were special costs at San Diego). But this is just for building the fence. The Corps of Engineers estimates that maintenance will run from $16.4 million to $70 million a mile over a twenty-five-year period—$32.8 billion to $140 billion for the entire fence.[19]

As of 2006, the U.S. government had 12,000 Border Patrol agents on the southwest border, at a cost of about $1.6 billion a year, with little effect on the flow of immigrants. What would it take for the U.S. military to seal off the border? Ten times the current number? This would mean 120,000 soldiers—a force almost as large as the one occupying Iraq as of 2006—at a cost of some $16 billion a year. And what would be their rules of engagement? Would they shoot to kill or maim, provoking an international outcry, as happened with the Berlin Wall?

"When policing is done by soldiers, our communities become the enemy," said Pedro Rios of the American Friends Service Committee's San Diego office, citing the May 1997 killing of eighteen-year-old high school student Esequiel Hernandez, Jr.[20] Hernandez was tending his family's goats in Redford, Texas, when he was shot and killed by one of four U.S. Marines on a Joint Task Force 6 anti-drug mission. The Marines, who were wearing heavy camouflage and armed with M-16s, claimed self-defense. But Hernandez probably didn't even see them—and certainly didn't realize they were soldiers—when he fired in their general direction with an eighty-year-old, 22-caliber rifle, which he used for target practice. His killing sparked an outcry, leading the Defense Department to suspend military missions on the border.[21]

How would smugglers deal with "sealed" borders?

There's no proof that sealing off the border would stop the flow of immigrants. Professor José Ramos of the Tijuana-based Colegio de la Frontera Norte expects smuggling organizations to "innovate, become more sophisticated, and for the migrant that will mean an even higher cost. It wouldn't surprise me if smugglers began crossing migrants through underground tunnels or began using boats."[22]

The use of tunnels to smuggle people and drugs has already become common; fifty such tunnels have been discovered along the Mexican border since 1990, and thirty-six of them between the fall of 2001 and the fall of 2006, according to Representative James Sensenbrenner, a Wisconsin Republican who supports tougher enforcement.[23]

Interestingly, the immigration enforcement agency doesn't seem to be focusing much on sophisticated smuggling operations. In fiscal year 2006, it began 299 human trafficking investigations that resulted in only 184 arrests.[24]

Increasing the number of low-paid guards at a border opens another avenue for illegal crossing. At least 200 U.S. public employees were charged between 2004 and 2006 with helping to move drugs or immigrants across the southwest border. Thousands more are under investigation. Criminal charges have been brought against Border Patrol agents, local police, a county sheriff, motor vehicle clerks, an FBI supervisor, immigration examiners, prison guards, school district officials, and uniformed personnel of every branch of the U.S. military, among others. James "Chip" Burrus, assistant director of the Criminal Investigative Division of the FBI, called the documented cases "the tip of the iceberg." "Nobody is seriously addressing corruption," complained Michael Maxwell, who resigned in 2006 as head of internal affairs for the U.S. Citizenship and Immigration Services bureau of the Department of Homeland Security. "The corruption is pervasive," Maxwell said; 3,000 allegations of misconduct, including 100 reports of bribery, remained uninvestigated when he left the agency.[25]

"A spike in corruption incidents would be expected with a combination of new recruits and higher smuggling fees and so on," explained Brown University professor Peter Andreas, co-author of *Policing the Globe,* a recent book on international crime. Since stepped-up border crackdowns have made the crossing more difficult and expensive, "[s]mugglers have more resources to use for corruption, and they have a greater incentive to devote money for corruption," Andreas said. T. J. Bonner, head of the union that represents Border Patrol agents, said poor screening of new recruits is partly to blame, as the agency tries to quickly hire more border guards. But James Tomsheck, head of the border agency's internal affairs division, noted that many of the agents arrested in the past two years were veterans on the job for many years. Tomsheck called the growing number of corruption cases "startling."[26]

Can't we cut off the "job magnet"?

Since unauthorized migrants come to the United States mainly to get work, many people argue that the best way to stop illegal immigration is to eliminate the job "magnet" that draws them here.

The "employer sanctions" included in the 1986 Immigration Reform and Control Act were supposed to accomplish that by making it much harder for employers to hire out-of-status immigrants. The law set up a procedure under which employers must require each new person they hire to show documents demonstrating eligibility to work legally in the United States. Employers who knowingly employ unauthorized immigrants may face fines of $275 to $11,000 per employee. A pattern of knowingly employing undocumented workers can result in a criminal fine of $3,000 and up to six months in jail.[27]

But the sanctions policy came with a loophole: employers are required to check the documents of new hires, but they don't have to verify that those documents are valid or legitimate. So the main result of the policy was a dramatic increase in the production and trade of false documents. When workers are found to have used false documents to get their jobs, it's the workers, not the employers, who are punished.

In 1999 the immigration agency issued just 417 "intent to fine notices" to employers for failure to comply with the 1986 law; by 2004 the number had dropped to three.[28] "Employers feel very strongly about maintaining access to immigrant workers and exert political pressure to prevent enforcement from being effective," University of California, San Diego economist Gordon H. Hanson told the *New York Times* in 2006.[29]

With undocumented immigration rising significantly since the 1986 law was passed, the government itself has had to acknowledge that the policy has been a failure. "[T]he widespread availability of false documents made it easy for unauthorized aliens to obtain jobs in the United States," Richard M. Stana of the U.S. Government Accountability Office (GAO) told Congress in June 2006. "In addition…some employers knowingly hire unauthorized workers, often to exploit the workers' low-cost labor."[30]

What have employer sanctions accomplished?

While employer sanctions have not kept employers from hiring out-of-status immigrants, they have made things worse for all workers by driving down wages and degrading working conditions. This effect was predicted: in November 1986, right after Congress passed employer sanctions, Mexican economist Rogelio Ramírez de la O warned that the United States would go on employing undocumented immigrants. "So the cost of this legislation is that for the illegal workers the salaries and working conditions will go down as the risk the employer takes becomes higher." It wasn't just economists who saw this. Gabriel Rocha García, a Mexican waiting to cross into the United States (and possibly an immigrant smuggler), told the *New York Times*: "[W]e will be hunted. The employers who are willing to hire us will take advantage of us. They will threaten to turn us in. They will want to pay us less because they will say they are taking a risk to give us jobs."[31]

Many employers have avoided sanctions by hiring their workers through subcontractors, so that the contractor rather than the employer is legally responsible if the workers are out of status. If one labor contractor gets shut down, another steps in and takes over the jobs, and the workers. "Employers in immigrant-heavy industries have shifted en masse to subcontracting in the wake of [the 1986 law]," Fordham Law School professor Jennifer Gordon testified before Congress in 2005. This practice is "[n]ow predominant in such industries as agriculture, janitorial, landscaping, and construction…" Gordon added that the practice "exerts downward pressure on wages in two ways. Contracts are put out to bid, encouraging contractors to offer the lowest possible price, which translates directly into falling wages. In addition, subcontracting introduces a middleman who takes a cut of the contract, further lowering the wages that workers receive. And of course, once subcontracting becomes the standard arrangement in any industry, its impact on wages affects all workers, documented or not, in that industry."

"Far from protecting U.S. workers, then," Gordon concluded, "employer sanctions lower their wages and undercut their efforts to obtain jobs and improve working conditions."[32]

The Basic Pilot Program was started in 1997 as a voluntary option for employers who want to comply with the 1986 law and don't want to hire unauthorized workers who present false documents. The program allows employers to check a worker's documentation online by matching it against the Social Security Administration (SSA) and Department of Homeland Security (DHS) databases via the Internet. But the program has a terrible track record of errors, and regularly reports that foreign-born workers are out of status when in fact their documents are in order. An independent evaluation of the program in 2002 concluded that the Basic Pilot Program "jeopardizes employee rights as defined by fair information standards." With authorized workers losing jobs because of inaccuracies in the program, a possible result is "growth in the underground economy, which could lead to worker exploitation and related problems," the evaluation noted.[33]

How are employer sanctions enforced?

The immigration agency's main tactic for enforcing employer sanctions has been workplace raids. These generally involve a scenario where agents arrive at a job site and arrest any workers who "look" foreign and who can't immediately prove they are authorized to be in the United States. Employers rarely face any consequences, while the workers are generally deported.

The government deemphasized workplace enforcement in 1999 after organizers raised public awareness of how the raids were hurting workers' rights. In 2002, the immigration agency brought back the raids with a new twist, capitalizing on public concern around security issues in the wake of the terror attacks of September 11, 2001. Airport workers—including those employed at fast-food joints in airport terminals—were the first to be targeted, followed by construction workers at military bases and others doing contract jobs at "sensitive" sites.

In April 2006, U.S. Immigration and Customs Enforcement (ICE), the agency in charge of interior enforcement, again shifted its focus, arresting 1,187 immigrant workers in a single day at more than forty plants of IFCO Systems North America, Inc., a pallet and crate manufacturer.[34] The agency claimed it was aiming at the employer, but as always, it was the workers and their families whose lives were devastated. The scale of the operation, and the government's announcement that more such raids were being planned, set off a wave of fear in immigrant communities—precisely at a moment when millions of immigrants and supporters around the country were organizing huge demonstrations to demand legalization and protest anti-immigrant legislation.[35]

How does workplace enforcement affect organizing?

While there's no evidence that workplace enforcement stops people from coming here, there's plenty of reason to think that it intimidates immigrant workers and makes it harder for them to successfully organize for better pay and working conditions. Workers frequently report that employees threaten to turn them over to immigration authorities if they try to stand up for their rights. "Immigration law is a tool of the employers," explained Cristina Vasquez, a former garment worker who became a regional manager for the garment workers' union, UNITE. "They're able to use it as a weapon to keep workers unorganized, and the [immigration agency] has helped them."[36]

In December 2004 the Co-Op coal mine in Emery County, Utah, fired at least twenty-five workers allegedly because the SSA and U.S. Citizenship and Immigration Services (USCIS) had ordered an investigation of their Social Security numbers. The firings preceded a union election scheduled for a week later; all the suspended workers were supporters of the United Mine Workers of America (UMWA), according to UMWA organizer Bob Butero. "This company has accepted their Social Security numbers for years," Butero said. "Is it by coincidence that now that these workers want to exercise their rights in a union election, they suddenly want to confirm [the numbers]?"[37]

If we make life hard enough for immigrants, will they leave?

Some opponents of immigration argue that the U.S. undocumented population could be reduced significantly through a strategy of attrition, in which we deport as many out-of-status immigrants as possible while making life so difficult for the rest that they will be compelled to leave. The plan would include increased raids and removals, mandatory workplace verification of immigration status, expanded use of state and local law officers to enforce immigration laws, the tracking of people entering and exiting the United States on temporary visas, and more state and local laws to discourage illegal settlement.[38]

Many of these measures are already under way, and are having an overwhelmingly negative impact on our society, while doing little or nothing to slow immigration. Some measures face serious opposition—for example, many local police departments object to enforcing immigration laws, since they don't want to discourage immigrants from reporting crimes or serving as witnesses.

In the end, heightened repression won't lead most immigrants to leave voluntarily. Some may return to their native countries if conditions there improve, as many young Irish immigrants have done in recent years.[39] For many immigrants, no matter how bad things get here, the situation in their country of birth is still worse. Some who do go back find that the economic crisis has deepened in their absence, and the money they saved working here isn't enough, so they have to return to the United States and try again. Others will stay here even if the situation improves in their native country—they have made the United States their home for years now, have raised U.S. citizen children, and have friends and family here. As of March 2005, an estimated 60 percent of undocumented immigrants had been in the United States for more than five years; 34 percent had been living here longer than ten years.[40]

Who profits from enforcement?

Companies profit indirectly from enforcement because it helps them to exploit workers and keep them from organizing. But immigration enforcement has also been a huge cash cow for many corporations. In September 2006, the aerospace and military company Boeing won a contract worth an estimated $2.5 billion to set up the "Secure Border Initiative Network" (SBInet), a web of new surveillance technology and sensors with real-time communications systems for the federal Customs and Border Protection (CBP) agency.[41] L-3 Communications won a contract worth $429 million to set up a border surveillance system. In May 2004, the Accenture company and its partners won a $10 billion contract to set up "US VISIT," an entry-exit tracking system for people visiting the United States.[42]

Such profitable contracts give large, powerful companies a strong financial incentive to lobby Congress for expanded enforcement.

10

What About "Guest Worker" and Amnesty Programs?

Are "guest worker" programs a solution?

The debate over immigration "reform" in the United States has included a lot of talk about expanding temporary worker or "guest worker" programs. These programs allow people to come here for temporary or seasonal jobs, and require them to go home when the job is done.

Temporary worker programs do nothing to resolve the status of millions of immigrants who have already established their lives here and want to stay. Such programs also create a sub-class of workers who are effectively unable to defend their rights. Some critics compare these programs to a modern form of slavery, because workers are generally not allowed to change jobs, and have no real way to fight back when they are cheated out of promised wages and faced with substandard living and working conditions.

Cecilio Santillana, a 78-year-old former "guest worker" from Mexico who picked beets, cherries, and cotton, and shoveled manure on farms across the United States in the 1940s and 1950s, told the *San Francisco Chronicle* why he opposed a temporary worker proposal that was included in an immigration bill the Senate passed in May 2006. "I'm against it, because they may do to the new workers what they did to us," he said. "We suffered a lot."[1]

Employers often claim that temporary worker programs are needed because a shortage of workers is hurting certain industries, especially farming. Labor rights activists disagree. "There are plenty of people who will do the job if you pay them enough," said José Oliva, director of the National Network of Workers Centers for the National Interfaith Committee for Worker Justice. "The pretension that there aren't enough workers here and you have to go and import them is just a way of expanding this slave labor program rather than paying decent wages."[2]

Some employers object to the rules and bureaucracy that come with temporary worker programs. Among other requirements, they must prove they can't find enough citizens or legal residents to fill the available jobs. Sometimes the workers themselves resist the restrictions imposed on them by these programs; they may try to escape and seek unauthorized employment with better pay and conditions.

Stricter enforcement is often used as a tool to weaken resistance to the temporary worker programs. Migrants are forced to choose between the substandard conditions of the temporary worker programs and the risks of working in the United States without legal status, under constant threat of arrest and deportation. Increased workplace enforcement also encourages employers to support temporary worker programs, as a way to avoid the raids while maintaining a captive labor pool they can easily control.

How did we end up with these "guest worker" programs?

The 1917 Immigration Act, passed in February of that year, barred immigrants from Asia but let in anyone from the Western Hemisphere who could pay a per-person "head tax" and pass a literacy test. The law also sought to ban the recruitment of foreign workers by denying admission to "persons...who have been induced...to migrate to this country by offers or promises of employment." In May 1917, one month after the United States officially entered the First World War, industry complaints about a farm labor shortage led the U.S. Department of Labor to set up a temporary worker program. The program suspended the head tax, the literacy test, and the bar on contract labor, allowing Mexican workers to enter the United States "for the purpose of accepting employment in agricultural pursuits." The program was later expanded to allow some non-agricultural work. Between 1917 and 1921, as many as 81,000 Mexican workers were admitted to the United States under the program.[3]

Temporary worker programs resumed during the Second World War. In 1942, the Mexican and U.S. governments worked out a deal for recruiting temporary field workers from Mexico. These workers became known as *braceros*—manual laborers, from the Spanish word for arms, *brazos*. Under pressure from the agricultural lobby, the arrangement with Mexico was extended several times until 1964. Under a similar deal starting in 1943, sugar companies in Florida brought in workers from the Caribbean colonies then known as the "British West Indies" (BWI). That agreement ended in 1947, but the Caribbean workers kept coming under international contracts allowed by the provisions of the 1917 Immigration Act.[4]

In 1952, the Immigration and Nationality Act established the H-2 visa category, setting new rules for the continuing admission of temporary laborers. In 1986, the Immigration Reform and Control Act (IRCA) expanded the H-2 program, creating the H-2A category specifically for agricultural workers and the H-2B category for workers in other "low-skill" industries.

Certain skilled workers like nurses or computer programmers can qualify for "specialty occupation" (H-1B) visas. They are generally paid less than U.S. workers doing the same jobs, but unlike H-2 workers, they are allowed to switch employers, and can be sponsored for green cards. There is an annual cap—set at 65,000 as of fiscal year 2007—on how many H-1B visas can be granted. The demand is such that the limit is reached months in advance. The cap on H-1B visas for fiscal year 2007, which started on Oct. 1, 2006, was reached by June 1, 2006.[5]

Slavery in the Cane Fields

In Florida's sugar cane fields, "guest worker" programs got their start in the early 1940s after African American cane-cutters fought back against slavery conditions on the sugar plantations. In the 1990 documentary H-2 Worker, filmmaker Stephanie Black interviewed one of these original workers, an African-American man named Samuel who started cutting cane in 1941, working out of the Bare Beach labor camp in Clewiston, Florida. Samuel described brutal conditions at the camp. "They'd wake us up around 2 or 3 o'clock," he told Black. "They had a shack-rouser... [and] if you didn't get up when the shack-rouser roused you...he'd come 'round with a cane knife and a blackjack, beating you out [of] bed, and as you run out the door there was one with a rifle making you get back in line. And you were guarded. I found that it was almost the same as a prison."

The workers were not allowed to leave, but Samuel decided to try. "On Christmas Day in 1941, I took a walk from the camp," he remembered. "I walked past them with the rifles, and hit the railroad tracks." Samuel walked more than sixteen miles to South Bay, where he reported the abuses at the labor camp. "And I finally got them to come in at night, and they caught these five camps with human beings locked up to the beds at night, and they found some of them were bruised and beat up."

In 1942, the U.S. Sugar Corporation was indicted for conspiracy to enslave African-American workers. The next year, the sugar companies started using "guest worker" programs to bring in cane cutters from the British West Indies.[6]

What happened to the Mexican "*braceros*"?

Temporary workers from Mexico had been actively recruited to work in the United States between 1917 and 1923, but after the Great Depression hit in 1929, Mexican workers suddenly made a convenient scapegoat. Arguing that the Mexicans were taking scarce jobs away from desperate U.S. workers, state and local authorities and the federal government launched a campaign against people of Mexican descent. Laws were passed barring the hiring of "aliens," and employers were urged not to hire anyone suspected of being of Mexican descent. As many as one to two million people of Mexican descent were deported or forced out of the United States between 1929 and 1944. Sixty percent of them were U.S. citizens, including many U.S.-born children of Mexican immigrants.[7]

In July 2003, the Mexican American Legal Defense and Education Fund (MALDEF) filed a lawsuit on behalf of Emilia Castaneda, who was born in Los Angeles in 1926 and forced to leave with her family when she was nine years old. The lawsuit has sought class action status to include other survivors of the sweeps. The state of California, the county of Los Angeles, the city of Los Angeles, and the Los Angeles Chamber of Commerce are named in the suit "because those entities were involved in a concerted effort to deport large numbers of Mexicans and also to create an atmosphere of fear," explained MALDEF lawyer Steve Reyes.[8]

In July 1942, as the Second World War started creating a new labor shortage, the United States and Mexico signed an agreement creating the Mexican Labor Program, popularly known as the *"bracero* program." The program grew quickly, from 4,203 workers in 1942[9] to 201,380 in 1953.[10] Most of the *braceros* worked in agriculture, or on the railroads.

In 1954, the government launched Operation Wetback, a massive deportation program geared at undocumented Mexicans. Starting in Texas in mid-July 1954, the crackdown targeted not only temporary workers or immigrants, but people of Mexican descent in general, including many U.S. citizens. Agents swarmed through Mexican-American neighborhoods, stopping anyone on the street who "looked Mexican," and asking them for identification.

The operation trailed off after a few months as funding began to run out, and public outrage over its civil rights violations sparked opposition in Mexico and the United States. No one really knows how many people were deported, though the immigration agency claimed as many as 1.3 million people were either deported or returned "voluntarily" to Mexico because they feared being picked up in the sweeps.[11]

The *bracero* program continued to grow throughout the crackdown, under pressure from the agricultural industry in the southwestern U.S. states. The number of workers logged as going through the program rose from over 300,000 in 1954 to over 400,000 each year from 1956 to 1959. The numbers started to drop in 1960, as Chicano activists (Mexican Americans who fought for civil rights) joined farm labor organizers—including César Chávez—in stepping up pressure on Congress to cancel the program, which was hurting their efforts to organize for better conditions in the fields. The program official-ly ended in 1964.[12]

From 1942 to 1949, 10 percent of *braceros'* wages were held in trust, alleged-ly to be deposited in savings accounts and reclaimed, with interest, when they returned to Mexico. The funds—totaling an estimated 60 million dollars—were to be transferred by Wells Fargo Bank to banks in Mexico, but somewhere along the way the money vanished, and the workers never got their pay. On April 5, 2001, a class-action lawsuit was filed in U.S. federal court in California against the U.S. government, the Mexican government, and three Mexican banks on behalf of several workers seeking to recover their lost wages. As of December 2006, the suit was on appeal in the Ninth Circuit Court of Appeals.[13]

In 2002, the Bracero Justice Act was introduced in the U.S. Congress in an effort to support the workers' claim, but the bill went nowhere. In Mexico, the former *braceros* have been fighting through the Congress and the courts, and with demonstrations in the streets, to reclaim their stolen pay. In 2005, the Mexican government announced it would pay roughly $3,800 to people who could prove their claim to the deducted pay, but the *braceros* say the amount is inadequate, and are continuing to fight for what is owed to them.[14]

How are "guest workers" treated now?

Workers who come to the United States with H-2 "guest worker" visas are generally signed up in their home countries by labor recruiters who make travel and visa arrangements. H-2B workers in particular are often charged exorbitant fees for visas, transportation and other costs, and many begin their employment indebted to recruiters, contractors, or employers. If the workers leave their jobs or get fired, they lose their visa status. Sometimes employers hold onto the workers' passports and other documents to keep them from leaving.[15]

In the H-2A program for agricultural workers, employers must provide workers with free housing—but the living quarters are often filthy, overcrowded, and otherwise inadequate. Employers are required to reimburse travel costs to the job site for H-2A workers who complete at least half the agreed-upon period of employment, and round-trip travel costs for workers who complete the full job period. Employers don't always comply with these rules. (In the H-2B program, employers don't have to provide housing or reimburse travel costs.)

H-2A workers are supposed to be paid a federally mandated state-by-state pay scale, known as the "adverse effect wage rate," which the Department of Labor sets above the local minimum wage to avoid depressing local pay. But employers routinely violate wage and overtime requirements, and workers are often cheated out of the pay they're promised.[16] In the film *H-2 Worker*, a timekeeper in the Florida sugarcane fields confessed that the bosses made him illegally alter documents to reflect fewer hours than the workers had actually labored. "It's very painful to know that a man is up there working all day, and only makes 16, or 18, or 21 dollars, and when his day is completed and he goes to his place of rest, he only go with three hours on his ticket. That's cruel."[17]

If workers want to keep their job, and want a chance at getting hired for the program again in the future, they stay quiet and put up with such abuses.[18] Farmers using the H-2A program "frequently violate the law," said Bruce Goldstein, executive director of the Farmworker Justice Fund in Washington. "And employers have tremendous bargaining power over workers who are too fearful to challenge unfair or illegal conduct."

Despite such drawbacks, there is tight competition for these jobs. Leticia Zavala, southern organizing director for the Farm Labor Organizing Committee (FLOC), said there is a waiting list of 17,000 Mexican workers who have come to North Carolina on the H-2A program in the past and would like to return.[19]

What happens when "guest workers" defend their rights?

Temporary workers are commonly told that if they speak to priests, legal aid attorneys, or union organizers, they'll be fired, deported, and blacklisted.[20] "Usually when [a guest worker] is seen talking to someone like me they're on a plane home the next day," said United Farm Workers (UFW) organizer Eric Nicholson.[21] As sugar farm supervisor Dale Kelly explained in the film *H-2 Worker*: "If we get some bad people, we just submit their names to the Jamaican government that we don't want them back, and they won't come back."

In November 1986, at least 100 sugarcane cutters at the Okeelanta Corporation in Florida stopped working to protest that the company was paying too little per row of cane and was falsifying their hours. The workers refused to go back to the fields until the hourly wage promised to them in the contract was honored. The company responded by bringing in Palm Beach County riot police agents with attack dogs and forcibly shipping the entire crew of H-2 workers—not only those who protested—back to Jamaica.[22] "People were running about, and when I look at the door, it was a policeman with a dog and a gun, ordering us to get out," one of the Okeelanta workers explained in *H-2 Worker*. "After I get out through the door, I seen another one with a gun holding me, ordering me to get on the bus." "Now they send 350 men home without time to gather their clothes or possessions," another worker explained. "Within a week's time the men were replaced with 350 other workers sent from the islands."[23]

In an effort to address such injustices, two unions recently negotiated contracts that cover H-2 workers. In September 2004, the Ohio-based FLOC signed agreements with the North Carolina Growers Association and the Mount Olive Pickle Company, settling a five-year boycott and extending union representation to more than 8,000 "guest workers" from Mexico.[24] In April 2006, the UFW signed a nationwide agreement with the international labor-contracting firm Global Horizons, after fighting the company for years over its abusive practices.[25]

However, these agreements remain controversial; many advocates question whether their protections can be enforced, given the built-in imbalances of temporary worker programs. Likewise, many people remain skeptical about efforts to include labor safeguards in proposed new "guest worker" legislation.

Do "guest worker" programs hurt U.S. workers?

Temporary labor programs push down wages and working conditions for everyone by creating a pool of workers who are unable to effectively defend their rights. In fact, employers have been the main force lobbying for "guest worker" programs, since these programs allow them to keep their labor costs down. But temporary worker programs aren't the only problem; laws and policies that deny legal status to immigrants have a similar negative impact on wages and working conditions.

The U.S. workers who are most affected by this "race to the bottom" are those who were already in the lowest-paid jobs—especially African Americans and U.S.-born Latinos. While some U.S. workers have turned their anger against immigrants, others have learned that by putting prejudices aside and overcoming language and cultural barriers, they can join together and organize to defend and expand their workplace rights. In Mississippi's poultry processing industry, for example, African-American workers have joined with recent immigrants from Latin America to form the Mississippi Poultry Workers Center, which brings their communities together to address unjust labor conditions.[26]

What's all this talk about amnesty?

An amnesty is generally a pardon granted to someone who has committed some kind of infraction. When talking about immigration, it usually means "forgiving" people either for having entered the United States without permission or for overstaying their visas, and granting them a way to remain here with permanent legal status.

Rights advocates sometimes prefer to use other terms, such as "legalization" or "regularization." Some dislike the word "amnesty" because it implies that out-of-status immigrants have done something wrong. As Los Angeles-based rapper Jae-P puts it in the song "¿Por Qué Me Tratas Así?" (Why do you treat me like that?):

I'm not looking for amnesty, I'm not a criminal
Why do I have to ask for a pardon, if I came to work?[27]

Regardless of how we say it, we're referring to the idea of providing some way for immigrants living here to gain legal status. Our immigration laws have become so harsh that there are millions of immigrants living here since the 1980s and 1990s who have no options at all to legalize their status. They include thousands of people who arrived here as children, who know no other country but the United States.

For over a decade, amnesty has been a rallying cry for immigrant communities. Immigrants are tired of being exploited, discriminated against, and treated as unwanted and disposable—even as the U.S. economy has grown to depend on their labor. A common chant in Spanish at immigrant marches is "*Aquí estamos, y no nos vamos*" (We are here, and we're not leaving).

Haven't we already had an amnesty?

As of 2006, the last immigrant amnesty in the United States was passed twenty years ago, as part of the 1986 Immigration Reform and Control Act (IRCA). That law allowed anyone who could prove they had been continuously present in the United States since at least 1982 to apply for permanent residency. Over 1.5 million people legalized their status through the 1986 amnesty. Nearly a million more won permanent residency through a "Special Agricultural Worker" program for migrants who had done at least ninety days of farm labor between May 1985 and May 1986.[28]

Other countries have approved amnesties more recently: in February 2005, Spain granted amnesty to immigrants who had been in the country at least six months, were employed, and had a clean record.[29] Some 550,000 people were legalized through the program in 2005.[30] Even before the amnesty, immigrants in Spain had options to gain legal status through family ties, employer sponsorship, or proof they had lived there for at least five years; in 2003 nearly 236,000 immigrants legalized their status this way.[31] Italy has had several amnesties for immigrants, although the number of people applying has always exceeded the number of residency permits available. In March 2006, more than 500,000 people lined up for just 180,000 permits.[32]

What impact will amnesty have in the United States now?

Granting legal status to undocumented immigrants is a necessary and positive step in correcting our unfair immigration policies. An amnesty will bring out-of-status immigrants out of the shadows, allowing them to reunite their families, avoid exploitation on the job, and get driver's licenses more easily. No longer trapped in a cash economy, they will be less vulnerable to muggings, and can report to police when they are victimized. As they become more settled, they will gain more economic stability.

With an amnesty, employers will have less excuse to pay workers "under the table" and cheat on taxes. Unions and workers' organizations will have greater success with campaigns that raise wages and improve labor conditions for everyone. The trade in false documents will drop off. Law enforcement agencies will stop wasting resources by targeting out-of-status immigrants. The travel industry will get a boost, since thousands of people who have been stuck here for years without status will finally be able to travel freely, within the United States and abroad.

Won't amnesty cause more problems later on?

Amnesty policies have their pitfalls. Since an amnesty is generally a one-time reprieve for immigrants already here, its impact is short-lived; within a few years, more immigrants have arrived and a new underclass of out-of-status people is created.

Also, dealmaking in Congress means amnesties often come packaged with stricter enforcement measures that counteract the positive effects of legalization and create new problems. For example, the 1986 amnesty came with "employer sanctions" that criminalized undocumented workers and did nothing to push employers to provide fair wages or safe working conditions.

An amnesty is necessary, but it has to be part of a comprehensive plan that provides an ongoing way for people to move across borders, addresses the root causes of migration, and upholds equal rights for all people regardless of where they were born.

11

Why Do We Jail and Deport Immigrants?

Who gets deported, and why?

Two 1996 immigration laws—the Illegal Immigration Reform and Immigrant Responsibility Act and the Antiterrorism and Effective Death Penalty Act—made deportation mandatory for many immigrants, stripping judges of their authority to determine whether someone should be allowed to stay in the United States. The new laws led to a dramatic increase in the number of people getting deported, from 69,680 in fiscal year 1996 to a high of 202,842 in fiscal year 2004. From fiscal years 1996 through 2006, more than 1.8 million immigrants were deported. While many are deported shortly after they arrive, at least a quarter of those deported in 2004 had been in the United States for more than a year when they were caught.

The 2004 total includes 41,752 "expedited removals"—81 percent of them involving Mexicans—under which people arriving in the United States are formally deported without a hearing. Not included in the total are 1,035,477 cases of "voluntary departure" and 378,130 "withdrawals of applications for admission" in fiscal year 2004; most of these involved Mexicans caught on the border and summarily returned to Mexico, without the penalties associated with formal deportations.[1]

Immigrants who get deported include:

- Immigrants caught entering the United States without permission.

- People caught in the interior of the country after either entering without permission, staying longer than allowed, or violating the conditions of their visa (by working without authorization, for example).

- People who stay in the United States after being ordered deported by an immigration judge, including asylum seekers whose petitions are denied. With new task forces rapidly expanding around the country, the immigration enforcement agency has stepped up its efforts to track down and arrest people it calls "fugitives" or "absconders"—even though because of the agency's frequent bureaucratic errors, some of them aren't even aware they were ever ordered deported.

- Immigrants convicted of crimes. This includes people who are deported as soon as they complete their jail sentences, as well as people who served out their jail or probation sentences many years ago. Many are long-term legal permanent residents. The immigration agency, with the help of local probation departments, has been systematically hunting down such immigrants—even those whose crimes were minor and who have complied with all parole, probation, and rehabilitation requirements. Immigrants with criminal convictions made up 21 percent of total deportees in 2004. Nearly 17 percent of them were convicted on criminal immigration charges; another 37.5 percent were convicted on drug charges.

What happens to people who are deported?

People who are deported are generally barred from returning to the United States for ten years. Some who have criminal convictions are barred for life. Waivers allowing deportees to return and reunite with their families here are granted only rarely, in very special cases.

Deportees face an uncertain future in their country of birth. Those who have spent most of their lives here usually have a very hard time adapting to a country they barely remember, or which has changed in their absence. Many have no family or friends in their "home" country, and may not even speak the language. The long-term prospects are not much better. Some people manage to adapt, but many don't, and even those with family support have a hard time. With few jobs available to them, some may get involved in gangs, drugs, or criminal activity. It's not surprising that many deportees try to return illegally to the United States, even though they face jail sentences for "illegal reentry" if caught.

What happens to the families of deportees?

Deportation is devastating to families. Longtime partners and children are often left behind, since the situation in the deportee's home country won't allow them to reunite there and survive economically. In interviews with 300 Salvadoran deportees, researchers collaborating with the resettlement assistance agency "Bienvenido a Casa" in El Salvador found that 52 percent of those deported had left a spouse or child in the United States, and that 38 percent of the deportees planned to return to the United States.[2]

Families left behind must struggle harder to survive without financial support, and may even have to send money to support the deportees. As of 1999, nearly one in ten U.S. households with children were of "mixed status," with at least one parent a non-citizen and at least one child a citizen.[3] (That figure is almost certainly higher today.) The deportation of a breadwinner can plunge children and partners who are U.S. citizens into sudden poverty, and force them to seek public benefits. To make matters worse, deportees lose any Social Security benefits they earned while working legally in the United States. Not even their U.S. citizen family members can collect.[4]

Families also suffer emotional trauma. "Letisha, Kristina, and Christopher ask for their dad everyday," says Barbara Facey, a member of the group Families for Freedom whose husband Howard was deported to Jamaica in 2003. "Their grades are dropping, and the school counselor says they are depressed. Childcare is really hard. When a family friend who was supposed to get Christopher from school was late a few times, the principal threatened to call Children's Services. With all this pressure, I don't have the time to properly treat my heart condition."[5]

What is immigration detention?

Immigration detention is the practice of jailing people the immigration author-ities are trying to deport. In some cases, the detainees are going through a legal process to see whether they can remain in the United States. Other detainees are simply being held until their deportation can be arranged.

The detainees are imprisoned as if they were being punished for a crime. But being present in the United States without permission is not a crime. It is a civil violation—the only one punished by confinement since debtor's prison was abolished in the nineteenth century. The courts argue that the administra-tive detention of immigrants isn't punishment, and no one has yet managed to successfully challenge the practice as unconstitutional.

If immigrant detainees were charged with a crime, they would be subject to regular court procedures, including the right to a court-appointed lawyer at public expense. But deportation hearings are civil court proceedings with fewer legal protections, and detainees are left to fight the charges on their own, unless they can afford a lawyer or can find one who will work for free. Their detention can last for years as cases wind through the immigration court system and are sometimes appealed to backlogged federal courts. Even after all appeals are exhausted, and a final deportation order is confirmed, many immigrants continue to sit in detention for months or years. Some immigrants don't even challenge their deportation yet remain jailed for years due to bureaucratic delays or problems getting travel documents.

Is immigration detention new?

Immigration detention has existed in the United States for over a century. The best-known detention center was the one at Ellis Island, where the U.S. gov-ernment processed arriving immigrants—and detained those deemed exclud-able—from 1892 to 1954.

In 1954, the U.S. government announced it would only detain immigrants in rare cases when an individual was considered likely to be a security threat or flight risk. Detention grew common again in the 1970s: from 1973 to 1980, the average daily number of people in immigration detention almost doubled, from

2,370 to 4,062. In 1981, mass detention was used to contain an exodus of "boat people" who reached the shores of Florida after fleeing turmoil in Haiti.[6]

In addition to stepping up deportations, the 1996 immigration laws subjected broad categories of immigrants to mandatory detention. Mandatory detention affects many asylum seekers and most people with prior criminal convictions, barring immigration judges from releasing them on bond.[7]

Who is in immigration detention, and where?

More than 230,000 people pass through immigration detention every year. About half are from Mexico; most of the rest are from other Latin American or Caribbean countries. Many have lived here for years, have U.S. citizen family members, and are deeply integrated into our society. About half of the detainees have criminal records.

Many asylum seekers, some of them torture survivors, are among the detainees.[8] The detainees also include children: 5,385 unaccompanied minors were detained over the course of 2001.[9] In May 2006 the Immigration and Customs Enforcement (ICE) agency opened a 500-bed jail in Texas just to hold families with children. Previously, when ICE arrested families with children it generally released them with orders to appear in court for deportation hearings. By August 2006, most such families were being detained instead of released.[10]

Detainees are held in federal immigration service processing centers, in facilities owned and operated by private prison companies, in federal penitentiaries and other Bureau of Prisons facilities, and in local jails around the country.[11] As of October 2006, ICE was using 165 facilities in forty-three states plus Puerto Rico and Guam to hold detainees for longer than seventy-two hours. (Other facilities exist that can hold detainees for less than three days.)[12]

A total of 235,247 people passed through immigration detention over the course of 2004, while the average daily detention population—the number of people in detention on any given day—was 21,919.[13] Late in fiscal year 2006, ICE added at least 6,300 new jail beds, and the number of detainees expanded rapidly.[14]

By the week ending July 31, 2006, the daily average number of detainees had reached 23,252, according to data obtained by advocates from the ICE

Detention and Removal Office. By the week ending August 31, that number was up to 26,100, and by the week ending September 30, 2006, it was 27,521.

The growth was almost entirely in what the agency refers to as "non-criminal" detainees. Such detainees made up 45.6 percent of the July 31 total; 49.6 percent of the August 31 total; and 52 percent of the September 30 total. The percentage of so-called "criminal offender" detainees (people with prior convictions) shrank correspondingly: they made up 44 percent of the total in July, 40 percent in August, and 37.7 percent in September. (The remaining detainees, categorized as "possible criminal," stayed between 10.3 percent and 10.4 percent of the total.)[15]

How long do people spend in detention?

Immigration detainees can be locked up for a few days, or for more than ten years. The average stay in detention seems to be about thirty-five days.[16] Mexicans generally spend the least amount of time in detention before being deported.[17]

For years, the government contended that it could hold detainees for as long as it took to deport them—for years or decades, or even indefinitely if it couldn't deport them. In the June 2001 *Zadvydas v. Davis* case, the Supreme Court limited such indefinite detention by setting a time frame of six months within which the immigration agency is supposed to deport people with final orders of removal. Unfortunately, the agency has tried to avoid complying with the ruling, and detainees usually have to sue the government in federal court to win their freedom. As of October 2006, according to government data, 10,875 people were still detained after receiving their final orders of deportation; of these, 991 had been held longer than the six months established under the *Zadvydas* ruling. Another 1,074 had been held longer than three months but less than six months.[18]

The American Civil Liberties Union (ACLU) of Southern California filed a class-action lawsuit in federal court on September 25, 2006, challenging the government's continuing defiance of the *Zadvydas* ruling. The immigration agency promptly freed two of the suit's six named plaintiffs. Fearing the suit would be voided if the rest were released, and realizing that many detainees don't have lawyers to help them sue, the ACLU included as additional plaintiffs all unknown detainees in the same circumstances.[19]

How bad is detention really?

Detainees are often subjected to arbitrary punishment, including shackling, solitary confinement, neglect of basic medical and hygienic needs, denial of outdoor recreation, and verbal, physical, and even sexual abuse.[20]

More than 57 percent of immigrant detainees are held in over 312 county and city prisons nationwide that have contracts with the immigration agency.[21] Women detainees are more likely than men to be placed in local jails—and mixed with the general prison population—because the immigration agency has less space reserved for women in its own service processing centers.[22] A 1998 Human Rights Watch report on immigration detainees held in local jails documented such problems as overcrowding, little or no outdoor exercise, insufficient access to legal representation, extreme room temperatures, vermin, inadequate medical care, food lacking in quantity and quality, and physical abuse.[23]

From 2001 through 2004, immigrants detained at the Passaic County Jail in Paterson, New Jersey, reported that they were systematically denied access to lawyers, mail, telephones, family, outdoor exercise, critical medical care, and edible food. A November 2004 National Public Radio report, based on a five-month probe by NPR journalist Daniel Zwerdling, exposed the repeated use of attack dogs to terrorize detainees at the jail; several detainees had to be treated for dog bites. After years of public outcry, Passaic's detention contract was terminated in 2006.[24]

In all the facilities that hold detainees, medical treatment is seriously inadequate. Most ailments are "treated" by detention center staff with aspirin. In Avoyelles Parish Prison in Louisiana, a Cuban detainee told Human Rights Watch: "One guy got pneumonia. He asked for medical treatment, and they put him in a lockdown cell. He never got medical treatment. He was in the lockdown room for a long time. He got skinny, skinny, then they let him go."[25] In another report for NPR, Zwerdling investigated the deaths of four people in immigration detention between May and November 2004; in all four cases, witnesses say the immigrants died after guards, prison medical staff, and/or immigration officers failed to respond appropriately to medical emergencies.[26]

At every jail Human Rights Watch visited for its 1998 report, detainees consistently reported that the only dental care offered was tooth extractions. In

Berks County Prison in Pennsylvania, Moroccan asylum seeker Musbah Abdulateef said he had ten teeth pulled in less than a year because the immigration agency would not approve the dental treatment he needed. He was having trouble eating and was anxious about his continuing dental problems.

The immigration agency often moves detainees around from jail to jail, often thousands of miles away, without informing their families or attorneys of their whereabouts, or allowing them to make a phone call. Detainees who complain to the press or organize protests are punished.

Detainee Ramón Medina told Human Rights Watch he was placed in solitary confinement at Pike County Jail in Pennsylvania after telling correctional officers he was going to file a complaint against them. Four guards took Medina to the solitary confinement cell with his hands and feet handcuffed and proceeded to beat him, leaving him with serious injuries.[27]

After leading a hunger strike at Passaic County Jail in January 2003, Palestinian activist Farouk Abdel-Muhti was transferred to York County Jail in Pennsylvania—177 miles from his attorneys and friends—and kept in solitary confinement there for eight months while his supporters carried on a campaign to free him. According to its own rules, the immigration agency was supposed to conduct a weekly review of its reasons for keeping a detainee in "segregation." When an attorney asked the immigration agency for its records of these reviews, the agency promptly moved Abdel-Muhti back to a New Jersey jail, where he was again placed with the general detainee population. Abdel-Muhti was held for two years in nine different jails and detention centers in three states before a federal judge finally ordered his release. Detention conditions, including frequent interruptions in his blood pressure and thyroid medications, caused his health to suffer. Abdel-Muhti died of a massive heart attack on July 21, 2004, just 100 days after he was freed.[28]

Detainees like Abdel-Muhti, with volunteer attorneys and support on the outside, have a better chance of getting out. There are not enough volunteer (pro bono) attorneys available, and most detainees don't have the resources to pay a lawyer to fight their case. (Attorney fees can easily run $20,000 for a deportation case.) Not surprisingly, 84 percent of detained immigrants are not represented by a lawyer.[29] The immigration agency gives detainees a list of legal service agencies to call, but not all the listed agencies can provide help, and some of the list information is incorrect or out of date.[30] Those who try to fight their cases alone may face language barriers, have little or no access to legal resources, and may be unfamiliar with complex immigration laws. Without legal representation, detained immigrants have scant hope of winning their cases.

Many detainees say the worst part of detention is not knowing how long it will last. Most prisoners serving sentences count the days until their scheduled release date, while most immigration detainees have no idea how long they will be held, and no way to find out.

For many of the detainees, including those who are eventually released, detention causes lasting trauma and emotional distress. For asylum seekers who have already suffered torture and abuse in their home countries, prison brings back old demons and sets back any chance at physical or emotional recovery. Studies on the detention of asylum seekers conducted by the U.S. Commission on International Religious Freedom, Physicians for Human Rights, and the Bellevue/New York University Program for Survivors of Torture have found disturbingly high levels of depression, anxiety, post-traumatic stress disorder, and worsened psychological health among detained asylum seekers.[31]

The Story of S.

S., an asylum seeker with no criminal record who had suffered repeated sexual and physical abuse throughout her childhood, was detained by the immigration agency for almost nine months in a county jail in upstate New York, alongside people arrested for child abuse, prostitution, and drug crimes. When friends came to visit S., her time in the visiting room would be interrupted every hour as guards took her out for routine strip searches, and made her spread her buttocks so they could visually inspect her anus. Her health deteriorated so much in detention that she was eventually taken to a local surgeon for a medical exam. "Because the surgeon works outside of the jail, in order to go see him I must wear leg irons, belly chains, handcuffs, and a handcuff box. It is very humiliating to be taken to a doctor's office and paraded through the front door in shackles in front of 8–12 other patients, but not as humiliating as being told to 'hurry up,' then falling over when I do (four days later my ankle is still swollen and bruised). Then when I got into the office and the doctor tried to do a physical exam, he couldn't because of the belly chains. The doctor did tell me (the officer wouldn't leave the room) that he wanted me to have a colonoscopy and a biopsy. But I was told that if I agree to have the procedure that officers from the jail would have to be present...I refused the procedure."

Thanks to pressure from attorneys, advocates, and elected officials, S. was freed in June 2004 and was allowed to live with friends while she appealed her asylum case. The day immigration officials released her, they didn't inform her attorneys or advocates; instead they left her on the street without even money for a phone call—breaking an earlier promise to let a local refugee service agency know so it could send someone to pick her up.[32]

How are families affected by detention?

Families suffer terribly when a loved one is detained. Already burdened by the family's loss of a wage earner, they must struggle to pay legal fees or find affordable help so their loved one can fight deportation. If the detainee is at a local jail, families wanting to talk via phone are generally stuck paying for exorbitant "prison collect" service. Rates vary depending on the phone company and the jail, but calls can run as much as $5 or more for the first minute, and eighty cents per additional minute, with call length often limited to fifteen or twenty minutes.[33]

Visits, when they are possible, are often traumatic, especially for children seeing a parent shackled and behind bars in a prison uniform. When detainees are moved to jails far from their homes, as happens frequently, most families can no longer visit. For a family already facing the prospect of a permanent separation, detention adds further stress, anxiety, and financial burden.

Is detention necessary?

The official purpose of detention is to prevent people from "absconding" by keeping them in jail until they are sent back to their countries of origin. The immigration agency also uses detention as a tool to pressure detainees to stop fighting their cases and accept deportation, as well as to discourage more people from seeking asylum in the United States. People who seek asylum are forced to choose between the prospect of sitting in U.S. jails for years and the persecution they fear at home.

Detention tips the scales of justice toward the government's side by making it harder for people to win their legal battles against deportation. Without detention, people arrested by immigration could remain with their families and in their jobs while they seek legal help to win their cases.

Would people really "abscond" if we got rid of detention? Under an alternative pilot program run by the Vera Institute of Justice, which provided immigrants facing deportation proceedings with legal information, referrals, and court date reminders, and required a community member to act as guarantor, between 88 percent and 94 percent of immigrants showed up for their first five court hearings. (This high rate of compliance is partly because participants who volunteered for the pilot program met certain selection criteria.)[34]

Does it really matter if people "abscond"? Is it worth the terrible human and financial costs of detention just to make sure "deportable" immigrants really leave the United States?

Who pays for detention — and who profits?

There are wide ranges in the daily cost of detaining an immigrant in federal facilities and local jails around the country. A July 2006 article in the *New York Times* reports that the average cost is currently about $95 per detainee per day.[35] With an average of 27,500 people in detention on any given day, that adds up to more than $953.6 million a year, paid for by our federal taxes.

For corporations, detention is a highly profitable and fast-growing industry. In January 2006, the Houston-based corporation KBR, a subsidiary of the oil and construction firm Halliburton, won an open-ended contract—potentially worth $385 million—to build temporary detention facilities in the event of an "immigration emergency." The company has strong ties to the White House.[36]

Revenues and stock prices continue to skyrocket for private prison companies building immigration prisons, like Corrections Corporation of America (CCA) and the GEO Group (formerly Wackenhut Corrections Corporation), a major transnational prison and security corporation. Between them, the two companies operate eight of the federal government's sixteen detention centers holding immigrants.

Private companies including CCA and GEO also manage many county jails, which currently hold 57 percent of immigration detainees. Federal immigration contracts generated about $95.2 million, or 8 percent, of CCA's $1.19 billion in revenue last year, and about $30.6 million, or 5 percent, of GEO's $612 million total income. In general, immigration detention contracts offer higher profit margins for private companies than regular prison contracts—in part because immigration detainees aren't provided with any of the education, recreation, treatment, and rehabilitation programs granted to other prisoners.[37] Even in jails that are managed by government agencies, there are private profits to be made in contracts for services including food, uniform laundering, and telephone calls.

Former top government officials also reap big profits from the detention and security business. The *New York Times* reported in June 2006 that at least ninety former officials at the Department of Homeland Security or the White House Office of Homeland Security—including Homeland Security Secretary Tom Ridge—had become executives, consultants, or lobbyists for companies that collectively do billions of dollars' worth of domestic security business. Among them was Victor X. Cerda, who in July 2005 left his job as acting director of Detention and Removal Operations for ICE, and was immediately hired by a law firm representing government contractors. One of his first lobbying clients was the GEO Group. While Cerda was still running detention operations for the government, a GEO Group subsidiary had won a contract to operate a 1,000-bed detention complex in Texas. Now Cerda helps GEO prepare new bids, the *Times* reported, and has even directly represented GEO in meetings with officials from his old department.[38]

12

Can We Open Our Borders?

What do we mean by open borders?

The term "open borders" can mean different things to different people, and it is often viewed in a negative light. But what we're talking about is freedom of movement—a basic human right.

Open borders usually mean the unrestricted movement of people between nations, but can also sometimes mean the free passage of material goods. Borders still exist, and each country has its own laws, government, and sovereignty. In some cases, no immigration or customs controls exist. In other cases, controls remain, but people are allowed to travel freely from one country to another.

Open borders can also mean a profit-driven model of "labor mobility," in which employers benefit from a large global pool of qualified workers competing for jobs. But under true freedom of movement, people aren't forced to travel long distances, leave loved ones behind, live as strangers in an unfamiliar place, and face discrimination in order to pull themselves and their families out of poverty.

Have any countries actually tried opening their borders?

The United States had an open immigration policy for nearly its first hundred years. Goods were subject to restrictions and tariffs, but people were free to immigrate. The first federal immigration law came in 1875, when Congress, under pressure from racists, began limiting the immigration of people from China. Later laws excluded all Chinese and set up a small entry tax (1882); created a literacy requirement and barred anarchists (1917–1918); and put strict limits on immigration from the Eastern Hemisphere (1924). People were completely free to cross the border from Mexico until the early 1900s.

Over the past twenty years, Europe has been moving toward establishing the free movement of people among its nations. Citizens of most European countries can travel freely throughout the region and work legally in any country. They can bring their families with them, and family members who are not European citizens can work legally too.[1]

Much of Western Europe has eliminated border checkpoints altogether. In 1985, France, Germany, Belgium, Luxembourg, and the Netherlands created a territory without internal borders—the "Schengen area," named for a town in Luxembourg where the first agreements were signed. Within the Schengen area there are no border controls: no one checks your documents as you enter one nation from another, and you don't even need a passport to travel. By the end of 2006, the Schengen area included thirteen European Union (EU) member nations, as well as Norway and Iceland, which are not part of the European Union. The United Kingdom and Ireland, both EU members, have not signed the Schengen agreement but have adopted some of its rules. Switzerland, which is not part of the European Union, plans to implement the agreement by 2008.

Ten nations that joined the European Union in 2004, and two others that joined in 2007, will be integrated gradually into the passport-free zone; in the meantime, their citizens can still travel freely throughout Europe by showing a passport.[2]

Across the Atlantic, two South American trade blocs—the Andean Community of Nations (CAN, including Bolivia, Colombia, Ecuador, and Peru) and the Southern Cone Common Market (Mercosur, including Brazil, Argentina, Uruguay, Paraguay, and Venezuela)—have been working toward eliminating travel and migration barriers between their member countries. The two blocs are eventually expected to merge and expand to include the remaining South American nations.[3]

In our increasingly globalized world, the expansion of freedom of movement is clearly under way. How we choose to adapt—by continuing to militarize our borders, or by learning to welcome and integrate newcomers—will shape our future as peoples, communities, and nations.

Does the European Union really have open borders?

Europe doesn't really have true freedom of movement—it still shuts out immigrants from outside the region. In fact, the EU countries have consolidated efforts to keep out immigrants from Africa and Asia under a policy popularly known as "Fortress Europe" which—similar to U.S. border policy—causes the deaths of hundreds of people each year who try to migrate. In 2005, a total of 673 migrants died en route to Europe, most of them Africans who drowned in the Mediterranean Sea while trying to reach Italy or Spain.[4] Like the United States, Europe has also faced criticism from international human rights organizations for its harsh policies toward migrants.[5]

A number of European countries have also restricted job access for migrants from the newer EU member states.[6]

Still, looking at the way Europe has been opening its internal borders gives us a window into what we might expect if we tried to open our own borders.

Has freedom of movement caused problems in Europe?

In a 2005 opinion survey, most EU citizens ranked "freedom to travel and work" as the European Union's most meaningful achievement.[7]

When the EU's border-free zone was first extended to Southern Europe in the early 1990s (Italy in 1990; Spain, Portugal, and Greece in 1992), many northern Europeans feared their countries would be flooded by people from the poorer southern nations who were seeking better-paying jobs. Some people did migrate in that direction, but as it turned out, many went the other way: retirees from Germany and the United Kingdom moved to Spain,

France, Greece, or Portugal in search of better weather and leisure conditions. Unemployment rates in most EU nations shrank between 1993 and 2002; unemployment in the region as a whole dropped by more than two percentage points.[8]

On May 1, 2004, eight Eastern European countries, along with the Mediterranean island nations of Cyprus and Malta, joined the European Union. These ten countries had a combined population of more than 100 million people with an average income roughly half that of the other European Union members.

The U.K. government, which put no restrictions on the new arrivals, had predicted that no more than 13,000 people would come each year from the new EU member states. But in the subsequent two years, about 500,000 Eastern Europeans registered as workers in the United Kingdom. The influx sparked public concern, leading Britain to impose restrictions on workers from Bulgaria and Romania, which joined the European Union as member states in 2007.[9]

But the feared economic consequences of mass migration from new EU member states to the more prosperous western European states have largely failed to materialize. "Although there will be continuing migration from east to west...geographical mobility within Europe has been, and is likely to remain, relatively low," the Ireland-based European Foundation for the Improvement of Living and Working Conditions concluded in an October 2006 report.[10]

Does freedom of movement threaten national identity or culture?

There is no reason to think that freedom of movement blurs the cultural lines between nations. Not counting the countries that joined the European Union in 2004 and 2007, most of the other EU member states have eliminated internal border controls and share a common currency, the Euro. Yet their separate national identities, languages, and cultures remain, apparently unaffected by their EU membership. No one thinks Spain and Sweden are the same country, or confuses Italy with Germany.

Migration and global trade have always existed; over the centuries some cultures have disappeared, but many more have remained. Even within national boundaries, distinct cultures can persist and thrive—as in India, a single nation where many different languages and cultural practices exist side by side—not always in harmony, but without losing their particular characteristics.

The adaptation of cultures to migration and globalization is inevitable. We can ease the transition by embracing a diversity of cultures and languages, and protecting and defending the rights of all people to maintain their cultural expressions.

How can we keep criminals and terrorists out without borders?

Since stricter immigration controls do nothing to prevent terrorism, we can logically expect that reducing or eliminating such controls won't make us more vulnerable to terrorist acts. The European Union has addressed safety concerns by increasing information sharing among member nations and expanding cooperation with non-member nations. A database has been created among the member nations that includes information about people's identities as well as stolen or lost items.

If we really had freedom of movement, some kinds of crime would virtually disappear—human trafficking and the false document trade, for example. Criminals and terrorists would no longer be able to blend into an underground world of out-of-status immigrant workers. And immigrant communities would be less afraid of collaborating with police to report serious threats.

Is opening the borders part of "free trade"?

Freedom of movement is a fundamental part of any economic integration plan in which the needs of people and communities are taken into account. Some efforts at "free trade" and economic integration have followed the European model, which includes free movement of people as well as goods, services, and money. But the United States created a very different model with the North American Free Trade Agreement (NAFTA), which took effect in 1994 between the United States, Canada, and Mexico. NAFTA allows corporations to move goods, services, and money across borders, but it shuts workers out. This kind of "free trade," which the United States has sought to expand into Central and South America, is not designed to benefit communities, but rather to help wealthy and powerful sectors increase their profits and build their political and economic muscle.

And while the European Union has worked to equalize economic conditions among its member nations in a "race to the top," NAFTA has done nothing to reduce the wage gap between the United States and Mexico. On the contrary, it has contributed to a "race to the bottom," which only benefits employers looking for cheap labor, and big companies looking for new markets. At the same time, NAFTA has had a devastating impact on small-scale farmers in Mexico, leaving them few options for survival, other than coming to the United States to work as undocumented immigrants.[11]

How would freedom of movement actually work here?

True freedom of movement would ideally be part of a collaboration among people throughout the world, geared toward lifting the standard of living for everyone and protecting human rights.

But as a first step, we could stop requiring people to get visas before coming to the United States. People arriving at airports and border crossings could get their passports stamped with an automatic unlimited entry visa, and would be provided with information about how to register to work here if they choose to. There would be a full and complete amnesty: no one would be disqualified from entry based on past "illegal" stays, deportations, or criminal records.

Those who want to work here could register online, via phone, or at a local labor office and could be granted a Social Security card immediately, along with information in appropriate languages, outlining the rights and responsibilities of workers and employers under U.S. law. (If you think the bureaucracy couldn't be that efficient, consider that for at least ten years the Internal Revenue Service has been providing instant Employer Identification Numbers to businesses or organizations that request them online or via phone, with a minimum of paperwork and hassle.)

Employer sanctions would be eliminated, and bosses wouldn't have to ask for documents other than the Social Security number (SSN) to set up payroll taxes. There could be a grace period, allowing immigrants to start working as soon as they arrived, as long as they apply for a Social Security number within a month of starting their job. At retirement age, anyone who has paid into the system could collect their social security earnings from wherever they happen to be living.

How would we control citizenship?

We could eliminate the category of permanent residency and let people apply directly for citizenship if they can show they have lived in the United States for at least thirty-six months over the past six years. (That would allow people to seek citizenship even if they spend only six months a year here.) Dual or multiple citizenship would be fully respected, and affirming U.S. citizenship wouldn't require anyone to renounce their citizenship elsewhere.

A citizenship test could focus on U.S. history (including the history of slavery and the civil rights movement), and basic rights and responsibilities (including labor rights) under U.S. law. The information needed to pass the test could be made available, in multiple languages, in free booklets and on the Internet. We could eliminate the English proficiency test, but take steps to ensure that free or low-cost classes in English and other languages are available to anyone who wants to learn—as part of a policy respecting the diversity of language and culture in our country.

What would happen if we opened the borders?

No one really knows exactly what would happen if we eliminated immigration restrictions, but we can speculate that we might:

- Save billions in tax dollars by reducing bureaucracy and ending immigration enforcement;
- Increase tax revenue by allowing more immigrants to work legally;

- Raise wages and improve working conditions by encouraging labor organizing;

- Boost the travel industry by allowing people to come and go as often as they want;

- Reduce violent crime by eliminating the fear that keeps victims from reporting it;

- Improve social and economic stability by allowing families to stay together;

- Eliminate the illegal trade in human trafficking and false documents.

Wouldn't we be flooded with immigrants?

Initially, if we opened our borders, we might see a lot of new immigrants arriving. But once people realize that everyone can come and go without problems, we might also see a large number of immigrants returning to their home countries for frequent or extended visits. New immigrants who come here to work would be able to save money sooner, rather than laboring for years just to pay off their debts to the smugglers who brought them here. Or people could choose to come here for seasonal or temporary jobs, and return home to spend the rest of the year with their families.

Even if there's an initial influx of immigrants, things would likely balance out fairly quickly. If so many people come that there aren't enough jobs to go around, some people will leave. (This country is an expensive place to live, especially if you're unemployed.) And if workers have a real choice about where they can live, factories overseas might be forced to raise wages or risk losing their employees.

Would our standard of living collapse?

Europe's standard of living certainly didn't collapse when the European Union opened borders between member states. In 1975, before the borders were opened, production workers in manufacturing in the original fifteen EU countries were making 80 percent as much as U.S. workers. By the 1990s they were generally making more than workers here—17 percent more in 2004.[12] From 1994 to 2003, the Gross Domestic Product (GDP) as measured in per capita purchasing power standards tended to equalize across the European Union, going slightly down in six of the region's wealthier countries and up in four, while generally rising in the poorer countries. Certainly, no European country saw its standard of living drop dramatically over the decade after the borders were opened.[13]

But when we talk about real freedom of movement, we are envisioning it as part of a global economic and social transformation that improves the standard of living for the world's poorest people and expands freedom and opportunity for everyone. Under a truly international open borders policy, migration could flow in all directions, so that workers dissatisfied with conditions in the United States could move to Europe to access higher wages, universal health care, and paid vacations. Already in 2005, a total of 4,300 U.S. citizens immigrated to Ireland, while only 1,700 Irish citizens came to the United States, according to Ireland's Trade and Employment Ministry.[14] When they retire, U.S. workers could move south of the border for better weather and cheaper housing, as many already do. (Of course, this should be a personal choice, not something people are forced to do because their pension income isn't enough to allow them to keep living here.)

Could freedom of movement really work?

Freedom of movement would work best if we improve education, protect labor rights and civil liberties, eliminate institutionalized racism and other forms of discrimination, and address other social inequalities. On an international level, we should promote policies that defend human rights, and ensure social justice and economic security. Instead of paying for wars, military occupations, and bank bailouts, we could devote our tax dollars to building a society where we could all realize our full potential.

But even without such changes, freedom of movement would be an improvement over what we have now. There's no reason to think it wouldn't work, and the potential advantages outweigh the risks. Why not try it?

Resources

If we believe our current immigration policy is unfair and needs to be changed, there are a few simple things we can do:

- Improve our understanding of the issues by seeking out information (the resources listed below are a good place to start).
- Talk to all kinds of people, learn from them, and share our own knowledge and experience.
- Get involved in an organization working for immigration reform, immigrant rights, or worker justice.

An expanded and updated version of the following list of resources is available on the website for this book: www.ThePoliticsofImmigration.org.

Suggested readings:

David Bacon, *The Children of NAFTA: Labor Wars on the U.S./Mexico Border* (Berkeley: University of California Press, 2004)

Justin Akers Chacón and Mike Davis, *No One Is Illegal* (Chicago: Haymarket Books, 2006)

Deepa Fernandes, *Targeted: National Security and the Business of Immigration* (New York: Seven Stories Press, 2006)

Bill Ong Hing, *Defining America through Immigration Policy* (Philadelphia: Temple University Press, 2004)

Rachel Meeropol, Barbara Olshansky, Michael Ratner, and Steven Macpherson Watt, *America's Disappeared: Secret Imprisonment, Detainees, and the "War on Terror"* (New York: Seven Stories Press, 2005)

John Ross, *The Annexation of Mexico* (Monroe, ME.: Common Courage Press, 1998)

Suggested films:

Abandoned: The Betrayal of America's Immigrants, directed by David Belle and Nicholas Wrathall (55 min. 2000) Bullfrog Films: www.bullfrogfilms.com/catalog/aban.html

Farmingville, directed by Carlos Sandoval and Catherine Tambini (78 min., 2003) Camino Bluff Productions, Inc.: http://www.FarmingvilleTheMovie.com

H-2 Worker, directed by Stephanie Black (70 min. 1990) Valley Filmworks, Inc.: www.lifeanddebt.org/h2worker/

Los Trabajadores/The Workers, directed by Heather Courtney (48 min. 2001) New Day Films: www.newday.com/films/Los_Trabajadores.html

Uprooted: Refugees of the Global Economy, directed by National Network for Immigrant and Refugee Rights (NNIRR) with Sasha Khokha, Ulla Nilsen, Jon Fromer, and Francisco Herrera (28 min. 2001) National Network for Immigrant and Refugee Rights: www.nnirr.org/get/get_video.html

Organizations:

American Friends Service Committee (afsc.org/immigrants-rights): Has a national program, Project Voice—Migration and Mobility Unit, that works to strengthen the voices of immigrant-led organizations in setting the national agenda for immigration policy and immigrants' rights.

American Immigration Lawyers Association (www.ailalawyer.com): A legal association for immigration attorneys with a membership of more than 10,000 immigration lawyers. AILA provides an immigration lawyer referral service on its website.

Border Action Network (www.borderaction.org): A network of immigrants and border residents in Nogales, Douglas, and Tucson, Arizona, working to amplify the voices and power of those who are most impacted by border and immigration policies.

Campaign for Labor Rights (www.clrlabor.org): Mobilizes grassroots support throughout the United States for campaigns to end labor rights violations around the world.

Coalición de Derechos Humanos (www.derechoshumanosaz.net): A grassroots organization working to promote respect for human and civil rights and to fight militarization, discrimination, and abuse of authority in the southern border region.

Coalition for Justice in the Maquiladoras (www.coalitionforjustice.info): A tri-national coalition of religious, environmental, labor, Latino, and women's organizations supporting worker and community struggles in the *maquiladora* industry.

Detention Watch Network (www.detentionwatchnetwork.org): A national coalition addressing the crisis of immigration detention and helping detainees and their loved ones make their voices heard.

Families for Freedom (www.familiesforfreedom.org): A multi-ethnic defense network by and for immigrants facing and fighting deportation.

Farmworker Justice (www.fwjustice.org): An organization working to empower migrant and seasonal farmworkers by improving their living and working conditions, immigration status, health, occupational safety, and access to justice.

Global Workers Justice Alliance (www.globalworkers.org): A cross-border network of worker advocates and resources that combats migrant worker exploitation by promoting portable justice for transnational migrants.

Immigration Equality (www.immigrationequality.org): A national organization working to end immigration discrimination against lesbian, gay, bisexual, transgender, and HIV-positive people, and to help win asylum for those persecuted based on sexual identity or HIV status.

Maquila Solidarity Network (www.maquilasolidarity.org): A labor and women's rights advocacy organization promoting solidarity with grassroots groups in Mexico, Central America, and Asia, that works to improve conditions in *maquiladora* factories and export processing zones.

National Employment Law Project (www.nelp.org): Provides information and advocacy in defense of low-wage workers, including immigrant workers.

National Immigration Law Center (www.nilc.org): Provides information, policy analysis, and advocacy in defense of low-income immigrants and their family members.

National Immigration Project (www.nationalimmigrationproject.org): A project of the National Lawyers' Guild, Inc. devoted to defending the rights of immigrants facing incarceration and deportation.

National Network for Immigrant and Refugee Rights (www.nnirr.org): A national organization bringing together immigrant, refugee, community, religious, civil rights, and labor organizations and activists from around the United States in defense of immigrant rights.

Rights Working Group (www.rightsworkinggroup.org): A nationwide coalition of groups and individuals committed to protecting civil liberties and human rights.

SweatFree Communities (www.sweatfree.org): A national network assisting sweatshop workers globally in their struggles to improve working conditions and form strong, independent unions.

U.S./Labor Education in the Americas Project (www.usleap.org): Works to support the basic rights of workers in Central America, Colombia, Ecuador, and Mexico, especially those who are employed directly or indirectly by U.S. companies.

United Students Against Sweatshops (www.studentsagainstsweatshops.org or www. unionvoice. org/studentsagainstsweat): An organization of students and community members at over 200 campuses around the United States, supporting the struggles of working people and challenging corporate power.

"Know-your-rights" information for immigrants:

American Civil Liberties Union (ACLU): ww.aclu.org/immigrants/gen/
    25251res20060421.html

American Friends Service Committee (AFSC): www.afsc.org/immigrants-rights/learn/
    KnowYourRights.htm

Fair Immigration Reform Movement: http://fairimmigration.org/learn/know-your-rights.html

Families for Freedom: www.familiesforfreedom.org/KYR.htm

Homies Unidos: www.datacenter.org/programs/homiesunidos-sp02.htm

National Employment Law Project: www.nelp.org/workers

National Immigration Law Center: www.nilc.org/ce/ceindex.htm#know-rights

National Lawyers Guild: www.nlg.org/resources/kyr/kyr_english.htm

Notes

Chapter 1: Who Are the Immigrants?

1. Pilar Mauler, "The Impact of Immigration Raid on Families," *Milwaukee Journal Sentinel*, August 10, 2006.

2. Eric Foner and John A. Garraty, eds., "Black Migration," *The Reader's Companion to American History*, Houghton Mifflin Company, 1991, accessed at Answers.com on February 22, 2007, http://www.answers.com/topic/black-migration.

3. Synopsis of "Underground Railroad," Historica Minutes, Historica Foundation of Canada website, http://www.histori.ca/minutes/minute.do?id=10166; "Commemorating the Underground Railroad in Canada," Parks Canada website, http://www.pc.gc.ca/canada/proj/cfc-ugrr/itm2-com/pg03_e.asp.

4. Jennifer Van Hook, Frank D. Bean, and Jeffrey Passel, "Unauthorized Migrants Living in the United States: A Mid-Decade Portrait," Migration Information Source (MIS), Migration Policy Institute (MPI), September 1, 2005, http://www.migrationinformation.org/feature/ print.cfm?ID=329.

5. Van Hook, Bean, and Passel, "Unauthorized Migrants Living in the United States."

6. Jeffrey S. Passel, "The Size and Characteristics of the Unauthorized Migrant Population in the U.S.: Estimates Based on the March 2005 Current Population Survey," Pew Hispanic Center, March 7, 2006, http://pewhispanic.org/reports/report.php?ReportID=61.

7. MPI Data Tools, August 12, 2006, http://www.migrationinformation.org/DataTools/graphs/.

8. Justin Akers Chacón and Mike Davis, *No One Is Illegal* (Chicago: Haymarket Books, 2006), 168; Jeffrey S. Passel, "Unauthorized Migrants: Numbers and Characteristics," Pew Hispanic Center, June 14, 2005, 30, http://pewhispanic.org/reports/report.php?ReportID=46.

9. Jeanne Batalova, "Spotlight on Legal Immigration to the United States," MIS-MPI, August 1, 2006, http://www.migrationinformation.org/feature/print.cfm?ID=414; Kelly Jefferys and Nancy Rytina, "U.S. Legal Permanent Residents: 2005," U.S. Department of Homeland Security, Office of Immigration Statistics, April 2006.

10. Sam Roberts, "The 300 Millionth Footprint on U.S. Soil," *New York Times*, October 8, 2006.

11. Van Hook, Bean, and Passel, "Unauthorized Migrants Living in the United States."

12. *Triennial Comprehensive Report on Immigration* (Washington, D.C.: Immigration and Naturalization Service, 2002), 36.

13. Van Hook, Bean, and Passel, "Unauthorized Migrants Living in the United States"; Passel, "The Size and Characteristics of the Unauthorized Migrant Population in the U.S."; Eduardo Porter, "Illegal Immigrants Bolstering Social Security with Billions," *New York Times*, April 5, 2005.

14. Vernon M. Briggs, Jr., *Mass Immigration and the National Interest: Policy Directions for the New Century*, 3rd ed. (Armonk, NY: M. E. Sharpe, 2003), 135.

15. Rick Lyman and Brenda Goodman, "New Data Shows Immigrants' Growth and Reach," *New York Times*, August 15, 2006.

16. MPI Data Tools, http://www.migrationinformation.org/DataTools/charts/final.immig. shtml.

17. Van Hook, Bean, and Passel, "Unauthorized Migrants Living in the United States."

18. Briggs, *Mass Immigration and the National Interest*, 48, 71.

19. Briggs, 70; U.S. Census Bureau 1910.

20. Briggs, 88–89.

21. Lyman and Goodman, "New Data Shows Immigrants' Growth and Reach."

22. David M. Reimers, *Still the Golden Door: The Third World Comes to America*, Second edition (New York: Columbia University Press, 1992), 220–223.

Chapter 2: Why Do People Immigrate?

1. Vernon M. Briggs, Jr., *Mass Immigration and the National Interest: Policy Directions for the New Century*, 3rd ed. (Armonk, NY: M. E. Sharpe, 2003), 51–53.

2. Carlos Sandoval and Catherine Tambini, *Farmingville*, 2003, http://www.Farmingville TheMovie.com.

3. Justin Akers Chacón and Mike Davis, *No One Is Illegal* (Chicago, IL: Haymarket Books, 2006), 109; James D. Cockcroft, *Mexico's Hope: An Encounter with Politics and History* (New York, NY: Monthly Review Press, 1998), 154; Tim L. Merrill and Ramón Miró, eds., *Mexico: A Country Study* (Washington, D.C.: GPO for the Library of Congress, 1996), http://countrystudies.us/mexico/53.htm; World Bank, World Development Indicators database, July 1, 2006, http://siteresources.worldbank.org/DATASTATISTICS/Resources/ GDP.pdf.

4. John Ross, *The Annexation of Mexico* (Monroe, ME: Common Courage Press, 1998), 174; Cockcroft, *Mexico's Hope*, 290–291, 210.

5. Deborah James, "Food Security, Farming, CAFTA and the WTO," undated—website page last updated September 13, 2005, http://www.globalexchange.org/campaigns/ cafta/background.html; "Mexico: Corn Shortage Forces Farm Shakeup," *Reuters*, October 23, 1995.

6. "En 8 Meses, 751,041 Trabajadores Quedaron Desempleados: Banxico," *La Jornada*, October 1, 1995; "Two Years Later, the Promises Used to Sell NAFTA Haven't Come True," *Wall Street Journal*, October 26, 1995.

7. Cockcroft, *Mexico's Hope*, 155.

8. "Indexes of Hourly Compensation Costs in U.S. Dollars for Production Workers in Manufacturing, 32 Countries or Areas and Selected Economic Groups 1975–2004," U.S. Department of Labor, Bureau of Labor Statistics, November 2005, ftp://ftp. bls.gov/pub/special.requests/ForeignLabor/ichccsuppt01.txt; David Bacon, *The Children of NAFTA: Labor Wars on the U.S./Mexico Border* (Berkeley and Los Angeles, CA: University of California Press, 2004), 53.

9. *Uprooted: Refugees of the Global Economy*, National Network for Immigrant and Refugee Rights, with Sasha Khokha, Ulla Nilsen, Jon Fromer, and Francisco Herrera (28 min., 2001); available at http://www.nnirr.org/get/get_video.html.

10. Akers Chacón and Davis, *No One Is Illegal*, 105.

11. Holly Sklar, *Washington's War on Nicaragua* (Boston, MA: South End Press, 1988), 64.

12. Sarah J. Mahler and Dusan Ugrina, "Central America: Crossroads of the Americas," Florida International University, published April 1, 2006 in Migration Information Source, a project of the Migration Policy Institute; http://www.migrationinformation. org/Feature/display.cfm?id=386.

13. Alexis Henríquez, "Los 20,000 Km Más Letales," *La Prensa Gráfica*, January 17, 2006, http://laprensa.com.sv/enfoques/394579.asp.

14. U.S. Agency for International Development (USAID) 2005 Budget: El Salvador, undated, http://www.usaid.gov/policy/budget/cbj2005/lac/sv.html.

15. U.S. Census Bureau, "Region and Country or Area of Birth of the Foreign Born Population, 1960 to 1990," http://www.census.gov/population/www/documentation/ twps0029/tab03.html; Megan Davy, "The Central American Foreign Born in the United States," Migration Policy Institute, April 1, 2006, http://www.migrationinformation. org/feature/print.cfm?ID=385.

16. Ruth Ellen Wasem, "U.S. Immigration Policy on Haitian Migrants," January 21, 2005, Congressional Research Service (CRS) Report for Congress, posted at http://trac. syr.edu/immigration/library/P959.pdf.

17. Kathleen Newland and Elizabeth Grieco, "Spotlight on Haitians in the United States," Migration Policy Institute, April 1, 2004, http://www.migrationinformation.org/feature/ print.cfm?ID=214; U.S. Census Bureau, 1990.

18. Sklar, *Washington's War on Nicaragua*, 192.

19. United Students Against Sweatshops (USAS) website, www.studentsagainstsweatshops. org (accessed December 2006).

20. David Gonzalez, "Latin Sweatshops Pressed by U.S. Campus Power," *New York Times*, April 4, 2003.

Chapter 3: Does the United States Welcome Refugees?

1. UNHCR website, http://www.unhcr.org: Basic Information about UNHCR, "Protecting Refugees—Questions & Answers," 2006 edition; Transactional Records Access Clearinghouse (TRAC) report, "Asylum Law, Asylum Seekers and Refugees: A Primer," August 7, 2006, http://trac.syr.edu/immigration/reports/161/; U.S. Citizenship and Immigration Services (USCIS) website, http://www.uscis.gov: "Asylee or Refugee Seeking Lawful Permanent Resident (LPR) Status" (from home page, follow links for "Services & Benefits," "Humanitarian Benefits," "Asylum," and "Asylee Adjustment to Permanent Resident Status").

2. Vernon M. Briggs, Jr., *Mass Immigration and the National Interest: Policy Directions for the New Century*, 3rd ed. (Armonk, NY: M. E. Sharpe, 2003), 95–96.

3. U.S. Holocaust Memorial Museum, "The Voyage of the *St. Louis*," http://ushmm.org/wlc/article.php?lang=en&ModuleId=10005267; Bill Ong Hing, Defining America Through Immigration Policy (Philadelphia: Temple University Press, 2004), 234–235.

4. Department of Homeland Security, "Yearbook of Immigration Statistics: 2005," Refugees and Asylees, Data Tables 13, 16.

5. "Judges Show Disparities in Denying Asylum," TRAC report, July 31, 2006, http://trac.syr.edu/immigration/reports/160/.

6. "Asylum Denial Rates by Nationality, FY 2000 - FY 2005," TRAC Immigration website, http://trac.syr.edu/immigration/reports/160/include/nat_denial_0005.html; Human Rights Overview: Columbia, January 18, 2006, Human Rights Watch website, http://hrw.org/english/docs/2006/01/18/colomb12206.htm; Human Rights Overview: Haiti, January 18, 2006, Human Rights Watch website, http://hrw.org/english/docs/2006/01/18/haiti12210.htm.

7. Ruth Ellen Wasem, "U.S. Immigration Policy on Haitian Migrants," Congressional Research Service (CRS) Report for Congress, updated January 21, 2005; Clifford Krauss, "U.S., in New Policy, Will Not Pick Up All Haiti Refugees," *New York Times*, May 22, 1992.

8. David G. Savage, "Haitian Intercept Policy Backed by High Court," *Los Angeles Times*, June 22, 1993.

9. Douglas Farah, "Coast Guard Patrols, Clinton's Switch on Repatriation Delay Haitian Exodus," *Washington Post*, January 21, 1993.

10. Susan Gzesh, "Central Americans and Asylum Policy in the Reagan Era," Migration Information Source, Migration Policy Institute, April 1, 2006, www.migrationinformation.org/Feature/display.cfm?ID=384; David M. Reimers, *Still the Golden Door: The Third World Comes to America*, Second edition (New York: Columbia University Press, 1992), 199–200; "ABC Class Members and NACARA," East Bay Sanctuary (Berkeley, CA), website, http://www.eastbaysanctuary.org/abcnacara.html (accessed October 2006; site disabled as of December 9, 2006).

11. "Equity of Relief," AILA (American Immigration Lawyers Association) Issue Paper (Doc. No. 21IP1004), June 14, 2001, posted on AILA InfoNet July 10, 2001, accessed at http://www.sackskolken.com/court/equity_relief.html.

12. Reimers, *Still the Golden Door*, 159B175; Briggs, *Mass Immigration and the National Interest*, 143–145.

Chapter 4: Why Can't They Just "Get Legal"?

1. Aarti Shahani, "Legalization and De-Legalization," *Gotham Gazette*, April 4, 2006, http://www.gothamgazette.com/article//20060404/11/1808.

2. "Multilingual Poll of Legal Immigrants On U.S. Immigration Policy," March 28, 2006, prepared by Bendixen and Associates for New American Media in partnership with LCCR (Leadership Conference on Civil Rights) Education Fund and Center for American Progress, http://www.civilrights.org/issues/immigration/details.cfm?id=41754.

3. Alison Siskin, Andorra Bruno, Blas Nunez-Neto, Lisa M. Seghetti, and Ruth Ellen Wasem, "Immigration Enforcement within the United States," Congressional Research Service Report, April 6, 2006, http://fpc.state.gov/documents/organization/64931.pdf.

4. Vernon M. Briggs, Jr., *Mass Immigration and the National Interest: Policy Directions for the New Century*, 3rd ed. (Armonk, NY: M. E. Sharpe, 2003), 129.

5. Thomas Alexander Aleinikoff, David A. Martin, and Hiroshi Motomura, *Immigration and Citizenship: Process and Policy* 4th ed., (St. Paul, MN: West Publishing Company, 1998), 295; as cited in Charles J. Ogletree, Jr., "America's Schizophrenic Immigration Policy: Race, Class, and Reason," *Boston College Law Review*, Volume 41, Number 4, July 2000.

6. State Department website: "2007 Diversity Visa Lottery Instructions," http://travel.state.gov/visa/immigrants/types/types_2645.html, "Diversity Visa Lottery 2007 Results," http://travel.state.gov/visa/immigrants/types/types_1317.html, both undated, both accessed December 9, 2006.

7. Mary Beth Sheridan, "15 Hijackers Obtained Visas in Saudi Arabia," *Washington Post*, October 31, 2001.

8. "Visas to the U.S.: How to Apply," U.S. Embassy, Mexico City website, undated, accessed December 9, 2006, http://mexico.usembassy.gov/mexico/evisas.html.

9. Philip Shenon, "Judge Denounces U.S. Visa Policies Based on Race or Looks," *New York Times*, January 23, 1998.

10. Table 6: Legal Permanent Resident Flow by Type and Major Class of Admission: Fiscal Years 1996 to 2005, Yearbook of Immigration Statistics: 2005, Department of Homeland Security (DHS), http://www.dhs.gov/ximgtn/statistics/publications/LPR05.shtm.

11. Jim Gardner, "Bring Me Your Rich, Yearning to Invest; Ex-Scourge of Illegal Aliens Now Bringing 'Yacht People' Ashore," *Orange County Business Journal*, July 20, 1992.

12. Walter F. Roche Jr. and Gary Cohn, "Immigration Official Insiders Siphon Millions Selling Green Cards to Wealthy Foreigners," *Baltimore Sun*, February 20, 2000.

13. Rebecca Daugherty, "Appeals Court Rules that Government Cannot Withhold Information on Official in the Name of Privacy," *The News Media & The Law* (Reporters Committee for Freedom of the Press), Winter 2003 (Vol. 27, No. 1), 26,

http://www.rcfp.org/news/mag/27-1/foi-appealsc.html; Walter F. Roche Jr., "Judges Rule for Release of Report in Visa Case. Ex-INS lawyer Virtue Accused of Favoritism in Investment Program," *Baltimore Sun*, November 26, 2002.

14. Kelly Jefferys and Nancy Rytina, "U.S. Legal Permanent Residents: 2005," Department of Homeland Security, Office of Immigration Statistics, Policy Directorate, Annual Flow Report, April 2006, http://www.dhs.gov/xlibrary/assets/statistics/publications/USLegal PermEst_5.pdf.

15. Rómulo E. Guevara, "Cutting Off Loose Ends: DOL Proposes to End Substitutions, Permanent Validity, and Improper Commerce of Labor Certifications," ILW.com, March 14, 2006, http://www.ilw.com/articles/2006,0314-guevara.shtm.

16. "Bona Fide Marriage Documentation," Immihelp.com: http://www.immihelp.com/greencard/bona-fide-marriage-documentation.html.

17. Carl Shusterman, Esq., "Till Death Do Us Part: Marriage & the Green Card," Immigration Issues at About.com.

18. "Family, Unvalued: Discrimination, Denial, and the Fate of Binational Same-Sex Couples under U.S. Law," Human Rights Watch and Immigration Equality Report, May 2006.

19. Richard Hanus, "Exceptional and Extremely Unusual Hardship: BIA Reverses Immigration Judge Ruling on an Undocumented Family of Six," Immigration Law Facts and Issues, September 26, 2002, http://www.usavisacounsel.com/article-51.htm.

20. Table 15, "FY 2005 Statistical Year Book," U.S. Department of Justice, Executive Office for Immigration Review (EOIR) Office of Planning, Analysis, & Technology, February 2006, http://www.usdoj.gov/eoir/statspub/fy05syb.pdf.

21. Based on authors' first-hand knowledge of the case.

22. "Southern Californians Demand Citizenship After Excessive Delays. Along with the ACLU and CAIR, Ten Area Residents File a Class Action Lawsuit," ACLU/SC News Release, August 1, 2006; "ACLU/SC Wins Citizenship for Seven. Class Action Lawsuit Challenging Naturalization Delays to Continue," ACLU/SC News Release, October 5, 2006.

Chapter 5: Is It Easy to Be "Illegal"?

1. Alfonso Chardy, "Fears of Mass Arrests Keep Undocumented Immigrants Off South Florida Streets," *Miami Herald*, April 27, 2006.

2. Kris Axtman, "Melting-Pot Cities Try New Police Tactics: Houston Cops Defy Convention to Solve Crime in Growing Immigrant Communities," *Christian Science Monitor*, August 28, 2002; Chris Echegaray, "Many Crimes Against Illegal Immigrants Go Unreported," *Tampa Tribune*, December 13, 2006.

3. Leslye E. Orloff and Nomi Dave, "Identifying Barriers: Survey of Immigrant Women and Domestic Violence in the D.C. Metropolitan Area," *Poverty and Race*, Vol. 6, Issue 4, August 31, 1997; Leslye E. Orloff and Rachel Little, "Somewhere to Turn: Making Domestic Violence Services Accessible to Battered Immigrant Women. A 'How To'

Manual for Battered Women's Advocates and Service Providers," Ayuda, Inc. (May 1999), chapter 13.

4. Alfonso A. Castillo, "Judge: Day Laborers' Rights Violated," *Newsday*, February 12, 2005.

5. "Hate Crimes," website of National Center for Victims of Crime, http://www.ncvc.org/ 9-11/main.aspx?dbName=hate_crimes, accessed February 12, 2007; Brad Knickerbocker, "National Acrimony and a Rise in Hate Crimes," *Christian Science Monitor*, June 3, 2005; Riad Z. Abdelkarim, "Surge in Hate Crimes Followed by Official U.S. Targeting of Muslim, Arab Men," *Washington Report on Middle East Affairs*, April 1, 2003.

6. Nicholas Riccardi, "Why Illegal Immigrants Fear Leaving: as Border Control Has Tightened, Many Have Sent for Their Families Instead of Risking a Visit," *Los Angeles Times*, April 12, 2006.

7. Heather Courtney, *Los Trabajadores/The Workers*, New Day Films, 2001, http://www.newday.com/films/Los_Trabajadores.html.

8. Tigres del Norte official band website: http://www.fonovisa.com/lostigresdelnorte.html; song lyrics translated from the original Spanish at http://www.lyricsdownload.com/ tigres-del-norte-los-la-jaula-de-oro-lyrics.html.

9. "Basic Facts about In-State Tuition for Undocumented Immigrant Students," National Immigration Law Center, April 2006 http://www.nilc.org/immlawpolicy/DREAM/in-state_tuition_basicfacts_041706.pdf.

10. Samuel G. Freedman, "Behind Top Student's Heartbreak, Illegal Immigrants' Nightmare," *New York Times*, September 1, 2004.

11. David Epstein, "Dream Deferred," *Inside Higher Ed*, July 28, 2006, http://insidehighered.com/news/2006/07/28/immigration.

12. Richard D. Vogel, "Harder Times: Undocumented Workers and the U.S. Informal Economy," *Monthly Review*, Volume 58, Number 3, July-August 2006; Roger Lowenstein, "The Immigration Equation," *New York Times Magazine*, July 9, 2006.

13. Robert Knox, "Undocumented and Unprotected: An Underground Economy of Improperly Classified Workers Cheats Laborers and Taxpayers Alike," *Boston Globe*, November 16, 2006.

14. Stephen Franklin and Darnell Little, "Fear of Retaliation Trumps Pain. Deaths, Injuries on the Job Soar for Illegal Immigrants," *Chicago Tribune*, September 3, 2006.

15. Thomas Maier, "Death on the Job: Immigrants at Risk" (five-part series), *Newsday* (Long Island), July 22-26, 2001, posted at http://www.publicintegrity.org/icij/award. aspx?act=2002; Katherine Loh and Scott Richardson, "Foreign-born Workers: Trends in Fatal Occupational Injuries, 1996–2001," *Monthly Labor Review*, June 2004, http://findarticles.com/p/articles/ mi_m1153/is_6_127/ai_n6179814/pg_1.

16. Franklin and Little, "Fear of Retaliation Trumps Pain."

17. "Exploiting workers," *Charlotte Observer* (editorial), September 17, 2006.

18. Workplace Fairness website, http://www.workplacefairness.org.

19. Rebecca Smith and Amy Sugimori (National Employment Law Project), and Ana Avendaño and Marielena Hincapié (National Immigration Law Center), "Undocumented Workers: Preserving Rights and Remedies after Hoffman Plastic Compounds v. NLRB," http://www.nelp.org/docUploads/wlghoff040303%2Epdf.

20. Mark Hamblett, "Judge Denies Clothier's Request to Obtain Workers' Immigration Files," *New York Law Journal,* June 18, 2002; *Zeng Liu, et al. v. Donna Karan International, Inc., et al.,* 00 Civ. 4221 (WK), 2002 U.S. Dist. LEXIS 10542 (June 11, 2002).

21. NILC Immigrants' Rights Update, Vol. 16, No. 6, October 21, 2002, http://www.nilc.org/immsemplymnt/emprights/emprights053.htm.

22. "EEOC Reaffirms Commitment to Protecting Undocumented Workers from Discrimination" (Press Release) June 28, 2002, http://www.eeoc.gov/press/6-28-02.html; EEOC Directives Transmittal #915.002, June 27, 2002, http://www.eeoc.gov/policy/docs/undoc-rescind.html.

23. Interview with Riva Enteen, Program Director at the San Francisco chapter of the National Lawyer's Guild, by GNN (Guerrilla News Network), undated, probably November 2002, posted at http://www.geocities.com/hal9000report/hal91.html.

24. Daniel González, " 'Wilson 4' Avoid Deportation: Judge Tosses Case over Profiling; Feds Plan Appeal," *Arizona Republic,* July 22, 2005.

Chapter 6: Are Immigrants Hurting Our Economy?

1. Commission on Behavioral and Social Sciences and Education (CBASSE), *The New Americans: Economic, Demographic, and Fiscal Effects of Immigration* (Washington, D.C.: The National Academies Press, 1997), 9-12, http://www.nap.edu/openbook/0309063566/html/219.html.

2. Testimony of Robert J. Rector before Senate Judiciary Subcommittee on Immigration, February 2, 1996, excerpted in *Melting Pot or Boiling Point? The Issues of Immigration* (Hudson, WI: Gary E. McCuen Publications, 1997), 78.

3. Shawn Fremstad, "Immigrants and Welfare Reauthorization," Center on Budget and Policy Priorities, February 4, 2002, http://www.cbpp.org/1-22-02tanf4.htm; Amanda Levinson, "Immigrants and Welfare Use," Migration Policy Institute, August 1, 2002, http://www.migrationinformation.org/USFocus/display.cfm?ID=45.

4. Eduardo Porter, "Illegal Immigrants Are Bolstering Social Security with Billions," *New York Times,* April 5, 2005; Jeffrey S. Passel, "The Size and Characteristics of the Unauthorized Migrant Population in the U.S.: Estimates Based on the March 2005 Current Population Survey," Pew Hispanic Center, March 7, 2006, http://pewhispanic.org/reports/ report.php?ReportID=61.

5. Justin Akers Chacón and Mike Davis, *No One Is Illegal* (Chicago, IL: Haymarket Books, 2006), 165B166; Porter, "Illegal Immigrants Are Bolstering Social Security With Billions"; Billy House, "Measure Bars Migrants From Social Security Pay," *Arizona*

Republic, June 26, 2005; Social Security Legislative Bulletin, March 4, 2004, http://www.ssa.gov/legislations/ legis_bulletin_030404.html.

6. Based on Internal Revenue Service 1040 form for 2005.

7. D. A. Barber, "The 'New' Economy?" *Tucson Weekly*, January 8, 2003, http://www.tusconweekly.com/gbase/Currents/Content?oid46422.

8. Levinson, "Immigrants and Welfare Use."

9. "Facts, Not Fiction: Common Myths about Immigrants," National Immigration Forum, August 4, 2006, http://www.immigrationforum.org/DesktopDefault.aspx?tabid=836.

10. Ruth E. Hernández Beltrán, "Still Unknown How Many Undocumented Immigrants Died in 9/11," *La Oferta* (San Jose, California) from Spanish news agency EFE, September 15, 2006.

11. Cara Buckley, "With Millions in 9/11 Payments, Bereaved Can't Buy Green Cards," *New York Times*, September 3, 2006.

12. Kevin O'Neil, "Remittances from the United States in Context," Migration Policy Institute, June 1, 2003, http://www.migrationinformation.org/feature/print.cfm?ID=138.

13. O'Neil; Akers Chacon and Davis, *No One Is Illegal*, p. 164.

14. Stephen Moore, Lowell Gallawy, and Richard Vedder, "Immigration and Unemployment: New Evidence," March 1994, quoted in *Melting Pot*, 103.

15. Rakesh Kochbar, "Growth in the Foreign-Born Workforce and Employment of the Native Born," Pew Hispanic Center, August 10, 2006, http://pewhispanic.org/reports/report.php?ReportID=69.

16. Testimony of James S. Holt before Subcommittee on Immigration and Claims of the House Judiciary Committee, December 7, 1995, excerpted in *Melting Pot*, 137–138.

17. Passel, "Size and Characteristics."

18. George J. Borjas, *Heaven's Door: Immigration Policy and the American Economy* (Princeton, NJ: Princeton University Press, 1999), 79, italics in original.

19. *The New Americans*, 6B7, 219–228.

20. Roger Lowenstein, "The Immigration Equation," *New York Times Magazine*, July 9, 2006.

21. Dean Calbreath, "Experts Say Exodus of Illegal Immigrants Could Stagger Economy," *San Diego Union-Tribune*, September 5, 2006.

22. Paul Krugman, "Wages, Wealth and Politics," *New York Times*, August 18, 2006; Steven Greenhouse and David Leonhardt, "Real Wages Fail to Match a Rise in Productivity," *New York Times*, August 28, 2006.

23. Calbreath, "Experts Say Exodus of Illegal Immigrants Could Stagger Economy"; Raul Hinojosa Ojeda, Robert McCleery, Enrico Marcelli, Fernando de Paolis, David Runsten, and Marysol Sanchez, "Comprehensive Migration Policy Reform in North America: The Key to Sustainable and Equitable Economic Integration," North American Integration and Development Center, School of Public Policy and Social Research, University of California, Los Angeles, August 29, 2001, 28, 30, http://naid.ucla.edu/ImmigReform83001.pdf.

24. David Bacon, *The Children of NAFTA: Labor Wars on the U.S./Mexico Border* (Berkeley and Los Angeles, CA: University of California Press, 2004), 284, 301.

Chapter 7: Is Immigration Bad for Our Health, Environment, or Culture?

1. Gorik Ooms and Ted Schrecker, "Expenditure Ceilings, Multilateral Financial Institutions, and the Health of Poor Populations," *The Lancet*, Vol. 365, No. 9473, May 21, 2005, 1821-1823; 50 Years Is Enough Network Fact Sheets: "Eliminating IMF and World Bank-promoted User Fees for Primary Health and Education," http://www.50years.org/action/s26/factsheet3.html and "The IMF, the World Bank and the HIV/AIDS Crisis," http://www.50years.org/action/s26/factsheet5.html.

2. National Coalition on Health Care website, www.nchc.org, accessed December 2006.

3. Evelyn Larrubia, "Illegal Immigrants' Healthcare Bill Is Tallied," *Los Angeles Times*, November 15, 2006.

4. U.S. Department of Health and Human Services, Centers for Disease Control and Prevention, Global Migration and Quarantine, "Communicable Diseases of Public Health Significance," http://www.cdc.gov/ncidod/dq/diseases.htm#communicable.

5. Donald G. McNeil Jr., "Where the Doctors Recognize Leprosy," *New York Times*, October 24, 2006; "Summary of Notifiable Diseases, United States, 2005," *Morbidity and Mortality Weekly Report* (published by Centers for Disease Control and Prevention), Vol. 54, No. 53, March 30, 2007 (for 2005), http://www.cdc.gov/mmwr/PDF/wk/mm5453.pdf.

6. "Trends in Tuberculosis—United States, 2005," *Morbidity and Mortality Weekly Report* Vol. 55, No. 11, March 24, 2006, 305-308.

7. Canada Communicable Diseases Report Volume 22S1, April 1996, http://www.phac-aspc.gc.ca/publicat/ccdr-rmtc/96vol22/22s1/22s1h_e.html.

8. Laura Beil, "The Infanct [sic] of AIDS Epidemic's Early Years Could Hold Clues to Disease's Future," *Dallas Morning News*, February 22, 1999.

9. Mark Fineman, "U.S. Bases, Politics Involved; Philippines Face Difficult Obstacles in AIDS Fight," *Los Angeles Times*, March 30, 1987.

10. Scott Long, Jessica Stern, and Adam Francoeur, "Family, Unvalued: Discrimination, Denial, and the Fate of Binational Same-Sex Couples under U.S. Law," Human Rights Watch/Immigration Equality report, May 2006, http://hrw.org/reports/2006/us0506/.

11. Haider Rizvi, "Border Fence Could Spell Environmental Disaster," published on Common Dreams, October 3, 2006, http://www.commondreams.org/headlines06/1003-08.htm.

12. Chris Clarke, "Immigration's Impact," *Earth Island Journal*, Vol. 21, No. 4, Autumn 2006.

13. Southwest Network for Environmental and Economic Justice, http://www.sneej.org.

14. "Invisible 5" website, http://www.invisible5.org/index.php?page=kettlemancity.

15. Cathi Tactaquin, "The Greening of the Anti-Immigrant Agenda," National Network for Immigrant and Refugee Rights, *Network News*, Spring 1998.

16. Committee on Women, Population and the Environment (CWPE), "Women, Population & the Environment: Call for a New Approach," presented at the United Nations Summit on Environment and Development in Rio de Janeiro, 1992, available on CWPE website, http://www.cwpe.org/.

17. "The State of Consumption Today," undated, Worldwatch Institute website, http://www.worldwatch.org/node/810; Nigel Purvis, "Greening U.S. Foreign Aid through the Millennium Challenge Account," Brookings Institution Policy Brief #119, June 2003, http://www.brookings.edu/comm/policybriefs/pb119.htm.

18. Project Censored, "U.S. Military's War on the Earth," http://www.projectcensored.org/publications/2004/15.html.

19. David M. Reimers, *Still the Golden Door: The Third World Comes to America*, 2nd ed. (New York, NY: Columbia University Press, 1992), 127; "La Población De México Alcanzó los 105.3 Millones a Mediados De Año," Secretaría de Gobernación (Mexico), July 20, 2004, http://www.gobernacion.gob.mx/templetas/boletin.php?id=3119; chart, INEGI—Instituto Nacional de Estadística Geografía e Informática (Mexico), July 19, 2006; eds. Tim L. Merrill and Ramón Miró, *Mexico: A Country Study* (Washington, D.C.: GPO for the Library of Congress, 1996), http://countrystudies.us/mexico/53.htm.

20. "Women, Population & the Environment: Call for a New Approach."

21. Brian Dixon, "Guest Opinion: Overpopulation the Cause of Common Problems," *Tucson Citizen*, November 16, 2006 (online edition); Population Connection Fact Sheet, "Population and Women's Empowerment," http://www.populationconnection.org/Communications/FactSheets/Womens%20Empowerment%202 002.pdf.

22. Kavitha Mediratta and Jessica Karp, "Parent Power and Urban School Reform: The Story of Mothers on the Move," Institute for Education and Social Policy, Steinhardt School of Education, New York University, September 2003; MOM website, http://www.mothersonthemove.org/.

23. Bill Ong Hing, *Defining America through Immigration Policy* (Philadelphia, PA: Temple University Press, 2004), 3.

24. Elizabeth Grieco, "English Abilities of the U.S. Foreign-Born Population," Migration Policy Institute, January 1, 2003, http://www.migrationinformation.org/feature/print.cfm?ID=84.

25. Testimony of John Trasviña, Interim President and General Counsel, Mexican American Legal Defense and Education Fund, at hearing of U.S. House of Representatives Committee on Education and the Workforce, Subcommittee on Education Reform, July 26, 2006, http://www.maldef.org/pdf/Trasvina_Testimony.7.26.06.pdf.

26. Justin Akers Chacón and Mike Davis, *No One Is Illegal* (Chicago, IL: Haymarket Books, 2006), 169.

27. Reimers, *Still the Golden Door*, 97, 129.

28. Commission on Behavioral and Social Sciences and Education (CBASSE), *The New Americans: Economic, Demographic, and Fiscal Effects of Immigration* (Washington, D.C.: The National Academies Press, 1997), 12–13.

29. Hing, *Defining America through Immigration Policy*, 28–50, 259–263.

30. Evelio Grillo, *Black Cuban, Black American* (Houston, TX: Arte Público Press, 2000).

31. John Ross, *The Annexation of Mexico* (Monroe, ME: Common Courage Press, 1998), 27–38.

Chapter 8: Are Immigrants a Threat?

1. "Immigration and the Justice System," *Research Perspectives on Migration*, a joint project of the International Migration Policy Program of the Carnegie Endowment for International Peace and the Urban Institute, Vol. 1, No. 5, July/August 1997, http://www.migrationpolicy.org/files/RPMVol1-No5.pdf.

2. Kristin F. Butcher and Anne Morrison Piehl, "Cross-City Evidence on the Relationship between Immigration and Crime," *Journal of Policy Analysis and Management*, Vol. 17, No. 3, 1998, 457–93.

3. Ted Chiricos and Sarah Eschholz, "The Racial and Ethnic Typification of Crime and the Criminal Typification of Race and Ethnicity in Local Television News," *Journal of Research in Crime and Delinquency*, Vol. 39, No. 4, 2002, 400–420.

4. Building Blocks for Youth reports: Eileen Poe-Yamagata and Michael A. Jones, "And Justice for Some," April 2000, http://www.buildingblocksforyouth.org/justiceforsome/; and Mark Soler, "Public Opinion on Youth, Crime and Race: A Guide for Advocates," October 2001, http://www.buildingblocksforyouth.org/advocacyguide.html.

5. Building Blocks for Youth report: Francisco A. Villarruel and Nancy E. Walker, "Donde Está la Justicia? A Call to Action on Behalf of Latino and Latina Youth in the U.S. Justice System," July 2002, http://www.buildingblocksforyouth.org/latino_rpt/index.html.

6. Sean Gardiner, "U.S. Deportation Policy," *Newsday* (Long Island, NY), April 4, 2004.

7. "September 11: More Effective Collaboration Could Enhance Charitable Organizations' Contributions in Disasters," United States General Accounting Office (GAO) Report to the Ranking Minority Member, Committee on Finance, U.S. Senate, December 2002, http://www.gao.gov/new.items/d03259.pdf; "List of Muslim Victims of September 11th Attack," compiled from the Islamic Circle of North America, *Newsday* victims database, and news reports, undated, http://islam.about.com/blvictims.htm.

8. Mary Beth Sheridan, "Immigration Law as Anti-Terrorism Tool," *Washington Post*, June 13, 2005; David Cole, "Are We Safer?," February 8, 2006, printed in *New York Review of Books*, Vol. 53, No. 4, March 9, 2006, http://www.nybooks.com/articles/18752.

9. "Terrorist Trials: A Report Card," Center on Law and Security, New York University School of Law, February 2005, http://www.lawandsecurity.org/publications/terroristtrialreportcard.pdf.

10. Cole, "Are We Safer?"

11. Coleen Rowley's letter, dated February 26, 2003, posted at http://foi.missouri.edu/whistleblowing/fulltextfbi.html.

12. Cole, "Are We Safer?"

13. *America's Challenge: Domestic Security, Civil Liberties, and National Unity After September 11*, Migration Policy Institute report by Muzaffar A. Chishti, Doris Meissner, Demetrios G. Papademetriou, Jay Peterzell, Michael J. Wishnie, Stephen W. Yale-Loehr, June 26, 2003, http://www.migrationpolicy.org/pubs/Americas_Challenges.pdf.

14. Mary Beth Sheridan, "15 Hijackers Obtained Visas in Saudi Arabia; Most Citizens of That Country Seeking to Visit U.S. Are Approved without Interviews," *Washington Post*, October 31, 2001.

15. "Border Security: Visa Process Should Be Strengthened as an Antiterrorism Tool," United States General Accounting Office Report to the Chairman, Subcommittee on National Security, Veterans Affairs, and International Relations, Committee on Government Reform, House of Representatives, October 2002.

16. Jim Lobe, "When Is a Terrorist 'Mastermind' Not a Terrorist?" InterPress Service/Global Information Network, October 25, 2006; Michael Fox, "Venezuela Demands Posada Carriles Extradition on 30th Anniversary of Bombing," Venezuelanalysis.com, October 9, 2006, http://www.venezuelanalysis.com/news.php?newsno=2099; Alfonso Chardy, "Judge: Posada Carriles' Time in Detention 'Well Beyond' Limit," *Miami Herald*, November 4, 2006.

17. Greg Palast report (transcript), BBC News "Newsnight," November 6, 2001, http://news.bbc.co.uk/1/hi/events/newsnight/1645527.stm; Alex Jones and Greg Palast, interview with Michael Springman (partial transcript), Alex Jones Radio Show, May 1, 2002, http://www.infowars.com/transcripts/springman.htm.

18. Michael Springman interview, July 3, 2002, on "Dispatches," hosted by Rick MacInnes-Rae on CBC Radio News (Canadian Broadcasting Corporation), http://radio.cbc.ca/programs/dispatches/audio/020116_springman.ram (unofficial transcript posted at http://911review.org/Wiki/SpringmanInterview.shtml).

19. Palast, BBC News, "Newsnight."

20. *Harpal Singh Cheema, Rajwinder Kaur v. Immigration and Naturalization Service*, No. 02-71311, December 1, 2003, http://www.ca9.uscourts.gov/ca9/newopinions.nsf/2494463A20ADD9FB88256DEF005C20C8/$file/0271311.pdf?openelement.

21. Camille T. Taiara, "After Years in Limbo—More Immigrant Detainees Choose 'Voluntary' Deportation," New American Media ("Disappeared in America" Series), August 7, 2006.

22. Pat McDonnell Twair, "Iranian Brothers' American Dream Turned Into a Nightmare" (Special Report), *Washington Report on Middle East Affairs*, July 2005, pages 44–45, 66, http://www.wrmea.com/archives/July_2005/0507044.html; Kelly Thornton, "Iranian Brothers Scarred by Accusations, Detention; 4 Held 3 1/2 Years in Los Angeles Jail," *San Diego Union-Tribune*, June 18, 2006.

23. Michael Isikoff, "Ashcroft's Baghdad Connection: Why the Attorney General and Others in Washington Have Backed a Terror Group with Ties to Iraq," Column (Web Exclusive), *Newsweek*, September 26, 2002, posted at http://www.truthout.org/ docs_02/09.30B. nswk.bagdad.htm; Michael Isikoff and Mark Hosenball, "Shades of Gray: The Duelfer Report Alleges that Saddam Gave Funds to a Listed Terror Group. But the Claim Does Little to Advance the White House Case for War," Column (Web Exclusive), *Newsweek*, October 17, 2004, http://www.msnbc.msn.com/id/6242223/site/newsweek/.

24. McDonnell Twair, "Iranian Brothers' American Dream Turned Into a Nightmare."

25. *America's Challenge*, Migration Policy Institute.

26. *America's Challenge*, Migration Policy Institute.

27. Jewish Virtual Library, http://www.jewishvirtuallibrary.org/jsource/Holocaust/ Niemoller_quote.html; webpage of Harold Marcuse, professor of German history at University of California, Santa Barbara, http://www.history.ucsb.edu/faculty/marcuse/ niem.htm.

28. *America's Challenge*, MPI.

29. Scott Long, Jessica Stern, and Adam Francoeur, "Family, Unvalued: Discrimination, Denial, and the Fate of Binational Same-Sex Couples under U.S. Law," Human Rights Watch/Immigration Equality report, May 2006, http://hrw.org/reports/2006/us0506/; Alicia J. Campi, "The McCarran-Walter Act: A Contradictory Legacy on Race, Quotas, and Ideology," American Immigration Law Foundation (AILF) Immigration Policy Brief, 2004, http://www.ailf.org/ipc/policy_reports_2004_mccarranwalter.asp.

30. "Chronology of the 'Los Angeles Eight' Deportation Case," Committee for Justice to Defend the Los Angeles Eight, http://www.committee4justice.com/chronology_ events.php.

31. William Branigin, "Secret U.S. Evidence Entangles Immigrants, Rarely Used Law Now Falls Most Heavily on Arabs," *Washington Post*, October 19, 1997.

32. Martin Merzer, "Muslim Cleric to Be Deported; Case Watched by Civil Libertarians," *Miami Herald*, August 19, 2002; "U.S. Deports Palestinian Detainee After Seven-Year Legal Fight," Associated Press, August 23, 2002.

33. David Cole, "National Security State," *The Nation*, November 29, 2001 (December 17, 2001 issue), http://www.thenation.com/doc/20011217/cole.

34. Jacqueline Charles, "Diplomats Puzzled by Claim Migrants Use Haiti to Enter U.S.," *Miami Herald*, April 25, 2003; "AG's Precedent Decision Denies Haitian's Release on Bond Based on Generalized National Security Concerns," NILC Immigrants' Rights Update, Vol. 17, No. 3, June 3, 2003, http://www.nilc.org/immlawpolicy/ arrestdet/ad065.htm; "Attorney General Ashcroft Calls for Blanket Detentions of Haitian Asylum Seekers. New Precedent Decision Portrays Haitians as Risks to National Security," Lawyers' Committee for Human Rights (now Human Rights First) Media Alert, April 25, 2003, http://www.humanrightsfirst.org/media/ 2003_alerts/ 0425.htm.

Chapter 9: Enforcement: Is It a Solution?

1. Adele Harrell, Shannon Cavanagh, and John Roman, "Evaluation of the D.C. Superior Court Drug Intervention Programs," National Institute of Justice (Washington, D.C.), Research in Brief, April 2000; Daniel Macallair, "Drug Use and Justice: An Examination of California Drug Policy Enforcement," Center on Juvenile and Criminal Justice (San Francisco, CA), October 2000.

2. Bill Ong Hing, *Defining America through Immigration Policy* (Philadelphia, PA: Temple University Press, 2004), 161, 165.

3. "Polling Summary: Public Support for Comprehensive Immigration Reform," National Immigration Forum, April 3, 2006, http://www.immigrationforum.org/DesktopDefault. aspx?tabid=808.

4. Russ Bynum, "Messy Aftermath of Immigration Raids Outrages Small Georgia Town," Associated Press, September 15, 2006.

5. Blas Nuñez-Neto, Stephen R. Viña, "Border Security: Fences along the U.S. International Border," Congressional Research Service (CRS), Library of Congress, September 15, 2006.

6. Hing, *Defining America through Immigration Policy*. 185–187.

7. Douglas S. Massey, "The Wall that Keeps Illegal Workers In," *New York Times*, April 4, 2006.

8. "President Bush's FY 2007 Budget for U.S. Customs and Border Protection (CBP) Totals $7.8 Billion," CBP fact sheet, February 7, 2006, http://www.cbp.gov/xp/cgov/ newsroom/fact_sheets/budget/bush 2007_budget.xml.

9. Olga R. Rodriguez, "New Wall Not Expected to Stop Migrants," Associated Press, October 6, 2006.

10. Hing, *Defining America through Immigration Policy*, 201.

11. Rodriguez, "New Wall Not Expected to Stop Migrants."

12. Rodriguez.

13. MPI Staff, "The US-Mexico Border," Migration Information Source, Migration Policy Institute, June 1, 2006, http://www.migrationinformation.org/Feature/display.cfm?id=407 (citing US Customs and Border Protection Public Affairs Office data).

14. Wayne Cornelius, "Evaluating Enhanced US Border Enforcement," Migration Information Source, Migration Policy Institute, May 1, 2004, www.migrationinformation. org/feature/print.cfm?ID=223.

15. Hing, *Defining America through Immigration Policy*, 199.

16. Douglas S. Massey, "Beyond the Border Buildup: Towards a New Approach to Mexico-U.S. Migration," *Immigration Policy in Focus*, Vol. 4, Issue 7, September 2005, http://www. ailf.org/ipc/policy_reports_2005_beyondborder.shtml.

17. Massey, "The Wall that Keeps Illegal Workers In."

18. Cornelius, "Evaluating Enhanced US Border Enforcement."

19. Blas Nuñez-Neto, Stephen R. Viña, "Border Security: Barriers along the U.S. International Border," Congressional Research Service (CRS), Library of Congress, September 21, 2006, 22.

20. "Border Communities and Migrant Families Used as Political Pawn by Administration Considering Troops on Border," American Friends Service Committee Press Release, May 12, 2006, http://www.afsc.org/news/2006/Bordercommunitiesandmigrantfamiliesused aspoliticalpawnbyAdministrationconsideringtroops.htm.

21. "D.A. Doubts Military Version of Border Shooting," Associated Press, June 4, 1997; "Grand Jury Doesn't Indict Marine in Border Shooting; Jurors Say Marines Followed Rules of Engagement," CNN, August 14, 1997, http://www.cnn.com/US/9708/14/ border.shooting/.

22. Rodriguez, "New Wall Not Expected to Stop Migrants."

23. Jim Abrams, "Immigration Bill Divides House, Senate," Associated Press, September 21, 2006, http://www.washingtonpost.com/wp-dyn/content/article/2006/09/21/AR200609 2100186.html.

24. Fact Sheet: ICE Accomplishments in Fiscal Year 2006, October 30, 2006, http://www. dhs.gov/xnews/releases/pr_1162228690102.shtm.

25. Ralph Vartabedian, Richard A. Serrano, and Richard Marosi, "Rise in Bribery Tests Integrity of Border," Los Angeles Times, October 24, 2006.

26. Onell R. Soto, "At Border, Rise Seen in Corrupt Workers," San Diego Union-Tribune, October 22, 2006, http://www.signonsandiego.com/uniontrib/20061022/news_ 1m22corrupt.html.

27. "Immigration Enforcement: Weaknesses Hinder Employment Verification and Worksite Enforcement Efforts," statement of U.S. Government Accountability Office (GAO) director for homeland security and justice Richard M. Stana to the Senate Committee on the Judiciary, June 19, 2006, 4–5.

28. "Immigration Enforcement," 15–17.

29. Eduardo Porter, "The Search for Illegal Immigrants Stops at the Workplace," New York Times, March 5, 2006.

30. "Immigration Enforcement," 7–8.

31. William Stockton, "Mexicans Expecting No Good of Immigration Law," New York Times, November 6, 1986.

32. "Lack of Worksite Enforcement and Employer Sanctions," hearing before Subcommittee on Immigration, Border Security, and Claims of the Committee on the Judiciary, House of Representatives, June 21, 2005; http://commdocs.house.gov/committees/judiciary/ hju21911.000/ hju21911_0.HTM.

33. Statement of Amy Sugimori, National Employment Law Project, before the Suffolk County Legislature Regular Meeting, September 5, 2006, citing Department of Homeland Security, Report to Congress on the Basic Pilot Program, June 2004, and Westat and Temple University Institute for Survey Research, Findings of the Basic Pilot Program Evaluation, summary and detailed reports, 2002.

34. "Hundreds Arrested in a Crackdown on Illegal Workers," Associated Press, April 20, 2006; "ICE Agents Arrest Seven Managers of Nationwide Pallet Company and 1,187 of the Firm's Illegal Alien Employees in 26 States," Immigration and Customs Enforcement (ICE) News Release, April 20, 2006.

35. Nina Bernstein, "Immigrants Panicked by Rumors of Raids," *New York Times*, April 29, 2006; Alfonso Chardy, "Fears of Mass Arrests Keep Undocumented Immigrants off South Florida Streets," *Miami Herald*, April 27, 2006; Miriam Jordan and Paulo Trevisani Jr., "Illegal Immigrants Skip Work Amid Unfounded Rumors of Government Roundup," *Wall Street Journal*, April 28, 2006; Miguel Perez and Elizabeth Llorente, "False Raid Rumors Spread, Panicking Local Immigrants," *Bergen Record*, April 27, 2006.

36. David Bacon, "The Law that Keeps Workers Chained," October 2, 1999, http://dbacon.igc.org/Imgrants/29ChainLaw.htm.

37. Glen Warchol, "Unions Denounce the Firing of Miners," *Salt Lake Tribune*, December 11, 2004.

38. Jessica M. Vaughan, "Attrition through Enforcement: A Cost-Effective Strategy to Shrink the Illegal Population," Center for Immigration Studies (CIS) Study, April 2006.

39. Katie Strang, "Immigration Hurdles Mark (Re)Turning Point for Irish," *Queens Chronicle*, November 2, 2006.

40. Jeffrey S. Passel, "The Size and Characteristics of the Unauthorized Migrant Population in the US: Estimates Based on the March 2005 Current Population Survey," Pew Hispanic Center, March 7, 2006, http://pewhispanic.org/reports/report.php?ReportID=61.

41. Alice Lipowicz, "Signed, Sealed, Delivered: Boeing Gets SBI-Net," *Washington Technology*, September 21, 2006; Joseph Richey, "Border for Sale: Privatizing Immigration Control," Corpwatch, July 5, 2006.

42. U.S. House of Representatives Committee on Oversight and Government Reform, "Dollars Not Sense: Government Contracting Under the Bush Administration," http://www.democrats.reform.house.gov/contracts.asp; "Homeland Security: Some Progress Made, but Many Challenges Remain on U.S. Visitor and Immigrant Status Indicator Technology Program," United States Government Accountability Office (GAO) Report to Congressional Committees, February 2005, http://www.gao. gov/new.items/d05202.pdf.

Chapter 10: What About "Guest Worker" and Amnesty Programs?

1. Tyche Hendricks, "Ex-Braceros Leery of Guest Worker Plan," *San Francisco Chronicle*, May 30, 2006.

2. Kari Lydersen, "Guest Workers Seek Global Horizons: U.S. Company Exploits Migrant Labor," CorpWatch, November 3, 2006, http://www.corpwatch.org/article.php?id=14216.

3. U.S. Commission on Immigration Reform, Binational Study: Migration Between Mexico and the United States, 1997: Vol. 1, Agustín Escobar Latapí, Philip Martin, Gustavo

López Castro, and Katharine Donato, "Factors that Influence Migration," http://www.utexas. edu/lbj/uscir/binpapers/v1-3latapi.pdf; Vol. 3, Philip Martin, "Guest Workers: Past and Present," http://www.utexas.edu/lbj/uscir/binpapers/v3a-3martin.pdf.

4. "Guestworker Programs for Low-Skilled Workers: Lessons from the Past and Warnings for the Future," Testimony before the Subcommittee on Immigration and Border Security of the Judiciary Committee of the U.S. Senate, February 5, 2004, Statement of Vernon M. Briggs, Jr., Professor of Labor Economics at the N.Y. State School of Labor and Industrial Relations at Cornell University, http://www.cis.org/articles/2004/briggstestimony020504.html.

5. "USCIS Reaches H-1B Cap," Department of Homeland Security, U.S. Citizenship and Immigration Services Press Release, June 1, 2006.

6. Stephanie Black, H-2 Worker, 1990, http://www.lifeanddebt.org/h2worker/.

7. Valerie Orleans, "Educator Brings Attention to Historic Period and Its Affect [sic] on Her Family," interview with Christine Valenciana, News and Information, March 17, 2005, website of California State University, Fullerton, http://campusapps. fullerton. edu/news/2005/valenciana.html (accessed December 6, 2006); Eric Roy, "Righting an Old Wrong," VOANews.com, posted September 29, 2003 at http://www.alternet. org/rights/16859/; Wendy Koch, "U.S. urged to apologize for 1930s deportations," USA TODAY, April 5, 2006, http://www.usatoday.com/news/nation/2006-04-04-1930s-deportees-cover_x.htm; California Senate Rules Committee, Senate Floor Analysis of SB 645, May 27, 2005, http://info.sen.ca.gov/ pub/05-06/bill/sen/sb_0601-0650/sb_645_cfa_ 20050527_150338_sen_floor.html.

8. Roy, "Righting an Old Wrong."

9. Daniel J. Tichenor, Dividing Lines: The Politics of Immigration Control in America (Princeton, NJ, and Oxford, UK: Princeton University Press, 2002), 210.

10. J. Craig Jenkins, "Push/Pull in Recent Mexican Migration to the U.S.," International Migration Review, Summer 1997, Vol. 11, No. 2, 183. (Table 2, data from U.S. Department of Justice Immigration and Naturalization Service).

11. Handbook of Texas Online, Texas State Historical Association website, http://www. tsha.utexas.edu/handbook/online/articles/OO/pqo1.html (accessed December 6, 2006).

12. David M. Reimers, Still the Golden Door: The Third World Comes to America, 2nd ed. (New York, NY: Columbia University Press, 1992), 38B40, 44, 54–55; John Ross, The Annexation of Mexico (Monroe, ME: Common Courage Press, 1998), 296–300; Jenkins, "Push/Pull in Recent Mexican Migration to the U.S."; David Bacon, "The Political Economy of Immigration Reform: The Corporate Campaign for a U.S. Guest Worker Program," Multinational Monitor, Vol. 25, No. 11 (November 2004), http:// multinationalmonitor. org/mm2004/112004/bacon.html; David Bacon, "Is a New Bracero Program in Our Future?" Z Magazine, October 2003, Vol. 16, No. 10, http:// zmagsite.zmag.org/Oct2003/bacon1003.html.

13. Website for attorneys Lieff, Cabraser, Heimann, & Bernstein, LLP, http://www. lieffcabraser.com/braceros.htm (accessed December 6, 2006).

14. Hendricks, "Ex-Braceros Leery of Guest Worker Plan."

15. "H-2B Program," Farmworker Justice website, http://www.fwjustice.org/Immigration_ Labor/H-2B.htm (accessed February 24, 2007); Tom Knudson, "Forest Guest Workers Tell of Abuses," *Sacramento Bee*, May 19, 2006; Danna Harman, "Guest Workers Vulnerable," *Christian Science Monitor*, April 25, 2006.

16. "The H-2A Temporary Foreign Agricultural Worker Program," Farmworker Justice website, http://www.fwjustice.org/Immigration_Labor/H2abDocs/H-2ASummary.doc (accessed February 24, 2007); "H-2B Program," Farmworker Justice website, http://fwjustice.org/ Immigration_Labor/H-2B.htm (accessed February 24, 2007); William G. Whittaker, "Farm Labor: The Adverse Effect Wage Rate (AEWR)," Congressional Research Service Report for Congress, April 14, 2005; Barry Yeoman, "Silence in the Fields," *Mother Jones*, January/February 2001, http://www.motherjones. com/news/feature/2001/01/farm.html.

17. Black, *H-2 Worker*.

18. Yeoman, "Silence in the Fields."

19. Eduardo Porter, "Who Will Work the Farms?" *New York Times*, March 23, 2006.

20. David Bacon, "Talking Points on Guest Workers," Truthout, July 13, 2005, http://www.truthout.org/cgi-bin/artman/exec/view.cgi/36/12611.

21. Lydersen, "Guest Workers Seek Global Horizons."

22. Marie Brenner, "In the Kingdom of Big Sugar," *Vanity Fair*, February 2001, http:// www.mariebrenner.com/articles/bigsugar/fan1.html; Black, *H-2 Worker*.

23. Black, *H-2 Worker*.

24. Steven Greenhouse, "North Carolina Growers' Group Signs Union Contract for Mexican Workers," *New York Times*, September 17, 2004; Paul Crowley, "Mt. Olive Boycott Officially Ends," Duke University *Chronicle*, September 17, 2004; "Precedent Setting Agreement Reached, Mt. Olive Pickle Boycott Over," Farm Labor Organizing Committee (FLOC) Press Release, September 16, 2004, http://www.floc.com/ presskit.html#olive.

25. Lydersen, "Guest Workers Seek Global Horizons."

26. Equal Justice Center, Poultry Worker Justice Project website, http://www.equaljusticecenter. org/PoultryWorker.htm (accessed December 6, 2006).

27. Jae-P, "¿Por Qué Me Tratas Así?" http://www.jae-p.com/. Lyric excerpt translated from the original Spanish by Jane Guskin. ("No busco amnistía, no soy criminal, por qué pedir perdón, si yo vine a trabajar.")

28. Vernon M. Briggs, *Mass Immigration and the National Interest: Policy Directions for the New Century* (Armonk, NY: M.E. Sharpe, 2003), 180, 183.

29. "España: Inmigrantes Ilegales Se Apuran a Pedir Residencia," VOA News, February 7, 2005; A. Agulló, "800.000 Inmigrantes Podrán Regularizarse a Partir de Hoy," 20minutos. es, February 7, 2005, http://www.20minutos.es/noticia/3446/0/inmigrantes/regularizar/.

30. "Más de 2,5 Millones de Inmigrantes Regularizados Hasta Septiembre," *Europa Press*, January 1, 2006.

31. "La Inmigración en Cifras," *El País* (Madrid), January 13, 2004.

32. Christian Fraser, "Italy Considers Immigrant Amnesty," BBC News, May 22, 2006.

Chapter 11: Why Do We Jail and Deport Immigrants?

1. Immigration and Customs Enforcement (ICE) Immigration Enforcement Initiatives Fact Sheet, June 23, 2006, http://www.ice.gov/pi/news/factsheets/immigration_enforcement_ initiatives.htm; Mary Dougherty, Denise Wilson, and Amy Wu, "Immigration Enforcement Actions: 2004," DHS Office of Immigration Statistics, Management Directorate, November 2005, http://www.dhs.gov/xlibrary/assets/statistics/publications/AnnualReportEnforcement 2004.pdf; Fact Sheet: ICE Accomplishments in Fiscal Year 2006, October 30, 2006, http://www.dhs.gov/xnews/releases/pr_1162228690102.shtm.

2. Scott Phillips, Jacqueline Maria Hagan, and Nestor Rodriguez, "Brutal Borders? Examining the Treatment of Deportees during Arrest and Detention," *Social Forces* 85.1 (2006), 93–109, University of North Carolina Press.

3. Michael E. Fix, Wendy Zimmermann, "All Under One Roof: Mixed-Status Families in an Era of Reform," Urban Institute Report, October 6, 1999, http://www.urban.org/ url.cfm?ID=409100.

4. Families for Freedom, "Myths & Facts," undated, accessed December 11, 2006, http:// familiesforfreedom.org/mythandfacts.htm.

5. Barbara Facey and Carol McDonald, "Bring Back Our Husbands," *ColorLines RaceWire*, posted on June 8, 2004 on Alternet.org, http://www.alternet.org/ story/18904/.

6. Mark Dow, *American Gulag, Inside U.S. Immigration Prisons* (Berkeley, CA: University of California Press, 2004), 6–7.

7. "Immigration Detention—An Overview," Detention Watch Network fact sheet, undated, http://detentionwatchnetwork.org/sites/detentionwatchnetwork.org/files/Detention%2 0Fact%20Sheet-%20Final%20for%20packet_0.doc; Families for Freedom website, "Definitions," accessed December 4, 2006, http://familiesforfreedom.org/ definitions.htm; "Mandatory Detention," United States Conference of Catholic Bishops, Office of Migration and Refugee Policy, at http://www.nccbuscc.org/ mrs/detention.shtml.

8. Dougherty, Wilson, and Wu, "Immigration Enforcement Actions: 2004"; Detention Watch Network, "Immigration Detention—An Overview."

9. "USA: Unaccompanied Children in Immigration Detention," Amnesty International USA Report, June 18, 2003, http://www.amnestyusa.org/refugee/pdfs/children_detention.pdf.

10. "ICE Accomplishments in Fiscal Year 2006," Immigration and Customs Enforcement Fact Sheet, October 30, 2006, http://www.dhs.gov/xnews/releases/pr_1162228690102.shtm.

11. Detention Watch Network, "Immigration Detention—An Overview."

12. ICE, "Authorized Detention Facilities—Over 72 Hours," list received from National Immigration Forum.

13. Dougherty, Wilson, and Wu, "Immigration Enforcement Actions: 2004"; Detention Watch Network, "Immigration Detention—An Overview."

14. "ICE Accomplishments in Fiscal Year 2006."

15. ICE chart: "Numbers of Detainees by Field Office," daily averages for weeks ending July 31, August 31, and September 30, 2006, provided by ICE to National Immigration Forum.

16. ICE chart: "Numbers of Aliens with Final Orders Detained by Field Office," October 2006, provided by ICE to National Immigration Forum.

17. Dougherty, Wilson, and Wu, "Immigration Enforcement Actions: 2004."

18. ICE chart: "Numbers of Aliens with Final Orders Detained by Field Office."

19. "ACLU Challenges Indefinite Detention in Southern California Facilities," ACLU News Release, October 9, 2006, http://www.aclu.org/safefree/detention/27048prs 20061009.html; Joe Mozingo, "Class-Action Suit Seeks Release of Detainees," *Los Angeles Times*, October 10, 2006.

20. Dow, *American Gulag*, 137.

21. David Crary, "Critics Decry Immigrant Detention Push," Associated Press, June 24, 2006, http://abcnews.go.com/US/wireStory?id=2115260&CMP=OTC-RSSFeeds0312.

22. Detention Watch Network, "Immigration Detention—An Overview."

23. "Locked Away: Immigration Detainees in Jails in the United States," Human Rights Watch report, September 1998, Vol. 10, No. 1 (G), http://www.hrw.org/reports98/us-immig/Ins989-05.htm.

24. Scott Lewis and Paromita Shah, "Detaining America's Immigrants: Is This the Best Solution?" Real Deal fact sheet produced by Detention Watch Network, the National Immigration Project, and the Rights Working Group, http://detentionwatchnetwork.org/sites/detentionwatchnetwork.org/files/R-D-1-Detention%20FINAL%20(2).pdf.

25. Human Rights Watch, "Locked Away: Immigration Detainees in Jails in the United States."

26. Daniel Zwerdling, "The Death of Richard Rust," National Public Radio (NPR) *All Things Considered* profile, December 5, 2005, http://www.npr.org/templates/story/story.php?storyId=5022866

27. Human Rights Watch, "Locked Away: Immigration Detainees in Jails in the United States."

28. First-hand knowledge based on authors' involvement in Abdel-Muhti's support team.

29. Lewis and Shah, "Detaining America's Immigrants: Is This the Best Solution?"

30. "USA: Amnesty International's Concerns Regarding Post September 11 Detentions in the USA," Amnesty International Report, March 14, 2002, http://web.amnesty.org/library/Index/engAMR510442002.

31. "From Persecution to Prison: The Health Consequences of Detention for Asylum Seekers," a Report by Physicians for Human Rights and the Bellevue/NYU Program for Survivors of Torture, June 2003, http://www.phrusa.org/campaigns/asylum_network/detention_execSummary/ detention_pdf.pdf; Craig Haney, "Conditions of Confinement for Detained Asylum Seekers Subject to Expedited Removal," in United States Commission on International Religious Freedom, Report on Asylum Seekers in Expedited Removal, Vol. II: Expert Reports, February 2005, http://www.uscirf.gov/countries/global/asylum_refugees/ 2005/february/conditionConfin.pdf.

32. Based on authors' letters and other communication with asylum-seeker "S.", her attorneys, elected officials, advocates, and immigration officials, January through June 2004.

33. First-hand knowledge based on authors' involvement in Abdel-Muhti's support team.

34. Oren Root, "The Appearance Assistance Program: An Alternative to Detention for Noncitizens in U.S. Immigration Removal Proceedings," Vera Institute of Justice, New York, http://www.vera.org/publication_pdf/aap_speech.pdf.

35. Meredith Kolodner, "Immigration Enforcement to Benefit Detention Companies," New York Times, July 19, 2006.

36. Katherine Hunt, "KBR Awarded Homeland Security Contract Worth up to $385M," MarketWatch, January 24, 2006.

37. Kolodner, "Immigration Enforcement to Benefit Detention Companies."

38. Eric Lipton, "Former Antiterror Officials Find Industry Pays Better," New York Times, June 18, 2006.

Chapter 12: Can We Open Our Borders?

1. European Union website: http://europa.eu/.

2. Website of the Schengen Visa: http://www.eurovisa.info/SchengenCountries.htm; Julia Gelatt, "Schengen and the Free Movement of People across Europe," Migration Policy Institute, Migration Information Source, October 1, 2005, www.migrationinformation.org/ Feature/display.cfm?id=338.

3. Mercosur website: http://www.mercosur.int; Comunidad Andina de Naciones website: http://www.comunidadandina.org/.

4. Data posted February 2006 by Gabriele del Grande on his Fortress Europe blog, http://fortresseurope.blogspot.com/2006/02/inmigrantes-muertos-en-la-frontera.html.

5. "EU: Protect the Rights of Migrants and Asylum Seekers in Seville Policy Proposals," Human Rights Watch Letter to EU Heads of State, June 13, 2002.

6. EURES, The European Job Mobility Portal, "About Living and Working," http://ec.europa.eu/eures/main.jsp?lang=en&acro=lw&catId=494.

7. "Mobility in Europe: Analysis of the 2005 Eurobarometer survey on geographical and labour market mobility," published October 23, 2006, by the European Foundation for the Improvement of Living and Working Conditions, http://www.eurofound. eu.int/pubdocs/2006/59/e/1/ef0659en.pdf.

8. Michael Braun and Camelia Arsene, "The Demographics of Movers and Stayers in the European Union," Final Conference, Pioneers of Europe's Integration "From Below": Mobility and the Emergence of European Identity among National and Foreign Citizens in the EU (PIONEUR) Project, Firenze, March 2006; "Intra-EU Migration: A Socio-Demographic Overview," PIONEUR Working Paper No. 3, July 2003, see http://www.obets.ua.es/pioneur/.

9. Sarah Lyall, "Britain to Restrict Workers from Bulgaria and Romania," *New York Times*, October 25, 2006 (Late Edition, A-6); Pavel Prikryl, "Bienvenidos, Still Not Willkommen: Europe Split over Labor Mobility Restrictions," Center for European Policy Analysis, June 6, 2006, http://cepa.ncpa.org/.

10. European Foundation for the Improvement of Living and Working Conditions, "Mobility in Europe."

11. Erica Dahl-Bredine, "U.S. Helped Create Migrant Flow," *National Catholic Reporter*, September 22, 2006, http://ncronline.org/NCR_Online/archives2/2006c/092206/092206w.php.

12. "Indexes of Hourly Compensation Costs in U.S. Dollars for Production Workers in Manufacturing, 32 Countries or Areas and Selected Economic Groups 1975-2004," U.S. Department of Labor, Bureau of Labor Statistics, November 2005, ftp://ftp.bls.gov/pub/special.requests/ForeignLabor/ichccsuppt01.txt.

13. PIONEUR, "Intra-EU Migration: A Socio-Demographic Overview."

14. "Ireland Considering Immigration Deal with U.S.," Reuters, October 25, 2006.

Index

LaVergne, TN USA
30 March 2011

222227LV00003B/14/P

3 4711 00208 3832

9 781583 671559